MEOW

Everything You Need to Know When Bringing a New Cat Home

Emma Barnes

Uranus Publishing

ISBN 978-1-915218-14-8

All rights reserved - © 2021 by Emma Barnes

This book is copyright protected. It is only for personal use. The content of this book may not be reproduced, duplicated or transmitted without direct written permission from the author or the publisher. All pictures contained in this book come from the author's archive or copyright-free stock websites (Pixabay, Pexel, Freepix, Unsplash, StockSnap, etc.).

Disclaimer Notice:

Please note the information contained within this document is for educational and entertainment purposes only. All effort has been executed to present accurate, up-to-date, reliable, complete information. No warranties of any kind are declared or implied. Readers acknowledge that the author is not engaged in rendering legal, financial, medical or professional advice. The content within this book has been derived from various sources. Please consult a licensed professional before attempting any techniques outlined in this book. By reading this document, the reader agrees that under no circumstances is the author responsible for any losses, direct or indirect, that are incurred as a result of the use of the information contained within this document, including, but not limited to, errors, omissions, or inaccuracies. The trademarks used are without any consent, and the publication of the trademark is without permission or backing by the trademark owner. All trademarks and brands within this book are for clarifying purposes only and are owned by the owners themselves, not affiliated with this document.

Contents

INTRODUCTION	1
1. THINKING OF GETTING A CAT?	5
2. LIVING WITH A CAT	15
3. PLAN AND PREPARE FOR YOUR NEW CAT	21
4. RAISING YOUR KITTEN	31
5. BASIC CAT TRAINING	45
6. UNDERSTANDING CAT BEHAVIORS	57
7. COMMON ISSUES WITH CATS AT HOME	85
8. TRAVELING WITH YOUR CAT	107
CONCLUSION	123

INTRODUCTION

Having a cat may be an enriching experience. A cat has the potential to relax your nervous system while also providing an immediate source of entertainment and play. Cats are independent animals who like scavenging and exploring on their own time, but they are also incredibly affectionate with their owners and anyone they trust.

To different people, having a cat can mean different things. Some people want a cat to snuggle and sit on their laps, while others prefer to live with a cat that spends most of its time outside and doesn't require a lot of human connection.

What matters is that you look for a cat who will interact with you if you want it to. All cats are not created equal, and how each one interacts with you is determined by its intrinsic personality and early experiences (or lack thereof), which can make it timid or confident around humans and in general.

The environment in which you maintain a cat is also quite important – if it lives with a lot of other cats that don't get along, for example, it will be anxious and respond differently than if it lived alone.

While there is no surefire way to find the perfect cat for you and your lifestyle, knowing your expectations and what makes cats tick will help you bring home a cat who will be able to adapt to its new surroundings and be the pet you desire.

You'll need to do the following to care for a cat:

- Provide a lot of human companionship
- Provide regular, appropriate meals as well as a steady supply of fresh water.
- Make sure the bed is clean and comfortable.
- Allow your cat access to the outdoors or be prepared to empty and clean a litter tray on a daily basis.
- Create a fascinating and safe atmosphere for it.

- Regularly groom it. Grooming is required daily for long-haired cats.
- Have it neutered between the ages of 4 and 6 months.
- Vaccinate your cat against the most common feline diseases regularly.
- Worm on a regular basis and treat for fleas.
- If your cat exhibits any signs of illness, take it to the clinic.
- Make sure you have insurance for your cat or that you can afford any veterinarian treatment it may require.

If this list has you discouraged or scared, don't worry. You don't have to give up on having a cat. I wrote this book thinking about everything I wanted to know before adopting my first cat. All the information you'll find in this book will save you a lot of trouble and wasted time. You'll learn how to deal with the most common situations in a cat's life and how to handle the unexpected. By following my step-by-step instructions, you will be able to enjoy your new four-legged friend in a carefree way.

If you purchased this book, it means your motivation is solid. So let's get started exploring the wonderful world of life with a feline. Happy reading.

Chapter One

THINKING OF GETTING A CAT?

Deciding to live with a pet is an important choice that must be made consciously. Indeed, if you are thinking about getting a cat, many questions will run through your head. I will try to answer the most common ones and clarify your ideas.

Is it possible to keep a cat indoor?

When you consider the life of a cat who has access to the outdoors, you'll see that being outside provides a lot of diversity and allows it to use all of its hunting behaviors if it wants to. Of course, there are dangers for cats outside, but you must weigh them against the benefits of physical and mental stimulation, as well as an outlet for natural behavior.

Should I get a kitten or an older cat?

A kitten allows you to adopt an animal from the start and treat and care for it to have the best possible start in life. You'll also be able to get a sense of its personality. On the other hand, Kittens take a lot of attention and planning to keep them out of danger. You must ensure that they are secure while away if you leave them alone. Depending on where you obtain your kitten, you may also need to arrange for neutering, initial vaccines, and other procedures.

While kittens have a high 'cute' factor, keep in mind that they only stay kittens for six months out of a potential lifespan of 14 years or more.

It's at least obvious when it comes to mature cats if they have long or short hair. You should get a good sense of a cat's personality, though if it is kept in less-than-ideal conditions and is anxious or afraid, it will act differently than when relaxed. A confident adult cat will likely move in and settle down immediately, whereas a scared adult cat may take longer. It will be much easier to leave an older cat alone knowing that it will not cause any problems, and it will be considerably less labor and stress than a kitten. A mature cat is almost certainly neutered and vaccinated.

Should I get a male or female cat?

It doesn't matter what a kitten's sex is as long as you neuter it before it enters puberty (about four months of age) when the impact of sex hormones kicks in. Cats who have not been neutered may engage in undesired reproductive behavior. Unneutered male cats, for example, would use strong-smelling urine to mark their territory, while unneutered female cats can come into season every two weeks if they do not become pregnant.

It doesn't matter whatever sex you acquire if you're only getting one cat or kitten. In the same way, if you want two kittens from the same litter, the sex of either cat is probably unimportant. However, if you already have a cat and are just getting one kitten or another cat, it would be worth considering obtaining one of the opposite sex to reduce rivalry. In such instances, a kitten may be a better option than another adult cat because the young cat's immaturity appears to remove the competition element - at least for a while. During this time, you hope they will get along! Neutering also eliminates the need for so much competitiveness and reduces the importance of sex.

Is it okay to keep a cat if I have a baby or small children?

If you have children, there is no reason not to have a cat or kitten. It is the responsibility of parents to teach their children from an early age how to approach, brush, and handle cats and treat them with kindness. Many children have wonderful connections with their cats and learn about respecting other animals and being nice — it happens all the time, but parents must set the standards. Taking on a new cat while also caring for a newborn or toddler might be a lot to handle at once, so making sure you have time for both parties is essential to a good connection. Similarly, there is no reason to get rid of the cat if you are pregnant. While the baby is young, simple hygiene precautions and common sense cat care can guarantee that everyone lives happily and safely together.

Is there a cat species that does not hunt?

You might have a strong aversion to your cat going outside to hunt. Perhaps you're a bird enthusiast, or you can't stand the sight of little carcasses on the floor. Hunting is a natural instinct for cats. While keeping a cat indoors may prevent it from killing anything, it will still require an outlet for this, its most basic behavior, and not all cats will thrive in this environment. Similarly, if you're just buying a cat to keep vermin at bay, you don't want to end up with one who isn't interested in hunting, shooting, or fishing and instead loves to sit on the couch! Older cats are less inclined to hunt than younger cats, and some cats don't bother at all, but it's impossible to predict how a cat will act.

Should I get a moggie or a specific breed?

The majority of cats kept as pets are moggies, or domestic short or long-haired cats, which are a random mix of several different cats whose parentage we have little knowledge of (well, the father anyway). This means we have no control over the kittens' color, body shape, coat length, or anything else their parents may pass on to them. If your kitten comes from a moggie mother but has an unknown father, it may acquire a longer coat than you want if the father was indeed long-haired.

There's more to picking a purebred cat than loving a certain coat color or length; some breeds have ethical issues to consider if you truly care about the cat's well-being. There are also health concerns to discuss with the breeder and questions to ask. Good breeders strive to produce healthy, people-friendly cats while avoiding (or attempting to address) any genetic diseases that may occur.

There are many different breeds, some of which will require extra care and attention, for example if they have a very long coat or even no coat at all. Some pedigree cats are more people-oriented and may not like to be left alone for long periods. If you are out all day at work, it may be worth getting two kittens together for company – do your research about the breed you are interested in. Always make sure that health comes first, no matter what the 'look'.

Should I get a male or female cat?

It doesn't matter what a kitten's sex is as long as you neuter it before it enters puberty (about four months of age), when the impact of sex hormones kicks in. Cats who have not been neutered may engage in undesired reproductive behavior.

Unneutered male cats, for example, would use strong-smelling urine to mark their territory, whilst unneutered female cats can come into season every two weeks if they do not become pregnant.

It doesn't matter whatever sex you acquire if you're only getting one cat or kitten. In the same way, if you want two kittens from the same litter, the sex of either cat is probably unimportant. However, if you already have a cat and are just getting one kitten or another cat, it would be worth considering obtaining one of the opposite sex to reduce rivalry. In such instances, a kitten may be a better option than another adult cat because the young cat's immaturity appears to remove the competition element - at least for a while, during which time you hope they will get along! Neutering also eliminates the need for so much competitiveness and reduces the importance of sex.

Is it okay if I have a dog and a cat?

Getting a cat should not be an issue if you already have other pets; you simply need to make sure that you evaluate everything. If you have a dog, make sure you make gentle introductions so your new cat does not get chased or damaged while the dog gets used to it. Not all canine breeds make suitable feline mates.

How many cats can I have together?

Cats are incredibly easy to 'collect' since they are addictively gorgeous, tiny, and easy to care for. Even if they don't get along, they are more likely to flee the situation than to fight.

However, there may be a lot of tension amongst cats that the owners aren't aware of. Cats are primarily solitary animals, and while they can live in groups, they are mainly made up of related individuals or are self-selected to ensure that cats do not share space with cats with whom they do not get along. Cats may begin to spray or soil in the house to cope with a situation in which they are stressed due to the presence of other cats, which may be the only thing that owners notice.

Thank your lucky stars and stop while you're ahead if you have three cats who get along swimmingly. If you already have two cats who get along swimmingly, think twice about adding another. Adding more cats may not just be the resident cats' relationship with the new one that creates problems. It may also upset the entire balance of the resident cats' relationship, causing problems even between the original cats as tension and stress levels grow. Any new cat should be introduced slowly and carefully.

Siblings are the best method to get two cats who get along. They'll have grown up together, which usually means a solid future relationship (but it's never guaranteed!).

How much does it cost to have a cat?

There will be charges associated with purchasing a pedigree cat, and these expenditures may be substantial. Pedigree kittens usually are vaccinated and neutered when they arrive. If you adopt a cat from a shelter, you may be asked to contribute or pay a fee, and the cat will almost certainly be neutered and vaccinated. Kittens or cats from friends or neighbors aren't usually neutered, vaccinated, wormed, or flea-treated, so you'll have to register with a vet and get these things done yourself. Although neutering is a one-time expense, a kitten will require several vaccinations to protect it from infectious diseases.

After that, a regular booster vaccination will help to protect it throughout its life (requirements vary depending on the cat's lifestyle and the risks associated with it – your veterinarian can advise you). Then there's food, flea, tick, and worm medication, cat litter if you want, or you require an indoor litter box, beds, and grooming tools if you get a long-haired cat. If your cat goes missing, microchipping is also recommended. We propose that you cover your cat as well, so that you are not responsible for any fees incurred in the event of an accident or illness. Select your insurance carefully to ensure that you get exactly what you want or need.

I have a cat allergy; is there a better breed than others?

Many people believe that cat hair causes us to sneeze, wheeze, or scratch when we come into contact with it. In fact, the allergy is caused by a protein or allergen called Fd1, which is found in feline saliva. Cats have saliva all over their coat because they groom themselves regularly. This dries on the cat's coat, and as it scratches, moves, or brushes past items, the dust or dander, as well as the allergen-containing hairs, are distributed around. Cat enthusiasts who truly want a cat but are allergic think they can circumvent the problem by choosing a breed with less, little, or no coat. However, because the condition is caused by saliva, this is unlikely to assist, and while long-haired cats appear to produce more allergic reactions, this is likely because they have more hair, which means they are exposed to more allergen.

It's recommended to visit friends with cats to test out different cats to see if they cause less of an allergic reaction. Unfortunately, persons who respond or have family members who are allergic have a tough time getting around.

What should I do with my cat while I'm away on vacation?

If you go on vacation, you must also consider who will care about your cat. If you're only going to be gone for a day or two, have a neighbor come in and feed it and check on it. If you are gone for longer than this, a boarding cattery might be a good option, as many cats will be searching for company. If your cat is scared, it may hide when the feeder arrives, and you won't be able to tell if everything is okay. A professional boarding cattery will keep your cat secure while you are away, and you will be able to relax. However, there are some poor boarding catteries.

Is it possible to feed a vegetarian diet to a cat?

Are you a vegetarian who wishes for your cat to follow suit? If you want a vegetarian pet that won't challenge your views, acquire a rabbit instead of a cat. Cats are carnivores first and foremost, and their appearance and behavior reflect this. A cat is an obligate carnivore, which means it has an absolute requirement for certain of the nutrients present in meat and all of its senses of smell and taste are oriented to being a carnivore; maintaining it as a vegetarian would be both unjust and detrimental to its health.

Is it time for me to buy a new cat?

If you're thinking of obtaining a new cat or kitten, pick a time when your house is peaceful (not during a family gathering, for example), and possibly a day or two when you can help it settle in and be there while it learns its way about, rather than shortly before you go on vacation.

Chapter Two

LIVING WITH A CAT

One of the reasons why so many people appreciate feline companionship is the adaptability of cat ownership. Cats make excellent pets for anyone who lives in a large house or a little apartment, and they provide all of the joy and entertainment that larger animal companions provide.

Why life is better with cats

If you're considering getting a cat, consider the following advantages:

Cats are easy to care for. Perhaps the most appealing feature of cats is that they require less upkeep and cost less than dogs, which require more exercise, training, grooming, toys, and care. Cats are also ideal for people who live in apartments or in cities. They don't need a lot of room to play and explore—navigating the nooks and crannies of your kitchen will keep them busy for hours.

They don't say anything. Cats meow when they're hungry, but you rarely have to worry about being startled awake or distracted from your work by a meowing cat. This makes them an excellent companion for people who work from home or have children who nap during the day.

They're self-sufficient. A cat will be there for you when you need them, but they can also keep themselves entertained. Most cats don't require or desire constant attention, and you'll never have to deal with guilt-inducing puppy eyes.

They keep pests out of your home. You're probably aware that cats enjoy hunting rodents. However, they're also natural insect killers, providing the kind of home security that Venus flytraps promise but rarely provide. Many cats like killing bugs like house flies and spiders, almost as if they are being compensated.

They live for a long time. Parting with your cherished pet is the most traumatic part of pet ownership. While you're still likely to outlive a cat, their longer lives allow you to spend more time with them—up to 20 years in some instances.

Health benefits

While every pet can give various health benefits, several advantages are unique to cats. They can:

Reduced anxiety and stress.

Cat owners are well aware of how a single session of petting or playing with their cats can transform a terrible day into a pleasant one. According to scientific studies, a cat's purr can help soothe your nervous system and lower your blood pressure.

Improve your heart and circulatory health.

It has been claimed that cat owners have a lower risk of heart disease and stroke.

Allergies can be avoided.

Cat hair is always mentioned as one of the most prevalent allergies. If a child is exposed to cats throughout their first few years of life, they are more likely to build an immune system that can fight cat allergies and other types of allergens.

Reduce your sense of isolation.

Cats make excellent pet companions. They provide unconditional love that rivals (and sometimes exceeds) that of many human companions and confidants.

How much care does a cat need?

Cats are low-maintenance pets compared to dogs, which require companionship, walking, and training, among other things. They do, however, require care, just like any other pet, and some cats require more care than others.

Do you want to spend a lot of time with your cat, or do you only have a limited amount of time? Cats are more adaptable to hectic, modern lifestyles than dogs since they are more independent, can be left alone more easily, and are better suited to smaller flats or houses. Cats are frequently chosen by people who have hectic and stressful lives and need company when they return home to unwind.

What do you hope to get out of your cat relationship? If you're the type of person who requires a close relationship with their cat and the ability to hold and engage with it, you'll be disappointed if you adopt a scared cat who hides every time you enter the room. You could wish to consider one of the pedigree breeds, which are more interactive and may require more human interaction than certain moggies. This could be a problem for the cat if you are at work all day and only have time to care for him in the evenings or on weekends.

To feel at ease, some cats need to know exactly what is going to happen when. Such cats might be quite content to live with an elderly lady who receives few guests and lives a very tranquil life, but they would likely find living in a home with children and other animals, as well as a lot of visitors and activity, to be rather stressful. On the other hand, other cats may thrive on a variety of contacts with a large number of people and would fit in wonderfully in a bustling household.

Don't get a Persian or a long-haired cat if you don't think you'll have the time or willingness to groom a cat daily. Any cat with a longer coat, other than a Persian, is referred to as semi-longhaired in pedigree jargon since the coat is not as full as a Persian's and does not have as thick an undercoat; nonetheless, it is still long and requires care. Furthermore, if you are particularly proud of your home, you may not want a lot of hair all over it.

A shorthaired cat is a lot easier to care for because most cats are obsessed with their coats and keep them in perfect shape. That isn't to suggest they don't shed hair - keep this in mind if you're considering a white cat but have dark furnishings or vice versa. A cat will also sharpen its claws indoors, most frequently on the stair carpet, occasionally on the furniture, and even on the wallpaper. There are things you can do to attempt to cope with this, but it's essential to realize from the start that your cat is an animal with free will and natural behavior that may not suit someone who requires a spotless home.

Chapter Three

PLAN AND PREPARE FOR YOUR NEW CAT

Cats make wonderful, affectionate family pets. However, you must be prepared when bringing your cat into your home for the first time. Getting a pet is a big responsibility, so having everything you'll need and preparing your home ahead of time is crucial.

Getting your house ready

Keep an eye out for strangling dangers. Cats are known for being curious and will play with whatever they can get their hands on. Look around your rooms for anything that could strangle you, such as the wires on your blinds.

If the cables are looped, try cutting them at the bottom or undoing the knot. Strangle-free blinds are currently being produced by several companies, as they are a hazard to children. Long drapes and tassels, as well as vertical blinds, can strangle your cat if its neck gets caught between the slats.

Look for any other potential dangers. Cats and kittens can be harmed by dangling wires, knickknacks, rubber bands, paper clips, and other small things. Consider securing cords with plastic tubing or placing them out of reach.

Rubber bands and paper clips should be stored in drawers or jars where your cat cannot access them. Knickknacks are more complicated. Although you can place them on higher shelves, cats are excellent jumpers. Some knickknacks might need to be hidden behind glass.

Keep the chemicals hidden. A variety of home toxins poisons cats. Consider cleaning products, insecticides, and automobile fluids, to name a few. All chemicals should be kept in cupboards where kitty will not be tempted to lick or drink them.

Some chemicals, such as some automobile fluids, have a delicious taste, attracting kittens to lick them. Another solution is to store them in locations where your cat is not permitted, such as the garage.

Harmful plants should be removed. A variety of common household plants poisons cats. You'd think your cat would know which plants to avoid, but cats are naturally curious and will munch on any plant they come across. Aloe, lilies, baby's breath, irises, and ivy are just a few examples of common hazardous plants.

Plants should be moved to higher ground or hung from the ceiling. Also, be cautious of falling leaves, as they might be poisonous. You can also take them outside or to a room where the cat does not go.

Make your cat a bed. If you want to keep your pet off the furniture, one method to help is to provide your cat with its particular beds. Even if you don't expect your cat to keep off the furniture, providing it with its bed can help it relax.

You'll need a bed in every room if you want the cat to keep off the furniture. It does not have to be a high-end cat bed. Even a beautiful, flat pillow or a folded blanket will suffice. Consider placing them in high-traffic areas where cats will enjoy them, such as on window sills.

Getting everything you need

Food, water, and litter, as well as containers. You'll need a container for food and a container for water. The easiest materials to clean include stainless steel, ceramic, and glass. A litter box and litter are also required.

Inquire about the food you're feeding your kitten or cat at the shelter where you got them, as it's best to start them on the same food.

Some cats dislike overly deep or narrow dishes, especially if their whiskers are constricted. At the very least, start with a small, shallow bowl.

Using the same type of litter in its new box can assist if you know what kind of litter the cat has previously used. Because some cats are picky about litter and litter boxes, you may need to experiment with a few different types before determining what your cat prefers.

Consider your cat's scratching and entertainment requirements. Toys help to keep your cat occupied. They can also serve as a diversion from ruining other items in your home. Make sure you have a variety of toys available, including jingly toys, string toys, and feather toys. In addition, rather than using your furniture to sharpen your cat's claws, you might wish to invest in a scratching post.

Scratching poles that are both robust and tall are the best. Because cats commonly stretch out to sharpen their claws, it should be at least long enough for the cat to stretch out full length and sharpen its claws.

Get a collar and an ID tag. An ID tag is vital because it allows people to find your cat if it runs away. If you've already decided, the ID tag should include the cat's name as well as some contact information for you, such as a phone number. Most pet stores feature tag-making equipment.

Choose a breakaway collar that will detach if snagged on something by your cat. The ID will be lost, but the collar will not strangle your cat.

A harness is another possibility. A harness features two loops: one around the cat's neck and the other beneath the first pair of legs. At least one strap runs down the back to connect the two loops, while a strap across the chest is also a nice option. Harnesses are preferable since they are less likely to strangle your cat and are more difficult to squirm out of.

Microchipping is a viable option. A microchip is a tiny chip (about the size of a grain of rice) implanted beneath your cat's skin. If your cat is taken to a shelter or a veterinarian, the microchip in their collar can be scanned to get your contact information.

Don't forget about the grooming equipment. Of course, you'll need a brush for your cat. Brushing your cat regularly is recommended for most cats, though the frequency depends on the sort of cat you have. To cut the cat's nails, you'll also need clippers. This is best accomplished with a pair of pet claw trimmers, which may be purchased at a pet store.

Find a veterinarian. Things happen, and your cat will become ill at times. When you do, it's a good idea to have a veterinarian on hand, so you have somewhere to take it. Ask your pet-owning friends for veterinarian referrals. It's also a good idea to visit the veterinarian to determine if you trust them.

You'll also want to get your cat vaccinated if it hasn't already, so having one in place when you bring your cat home is a good idea.

If your cat hasn't previously been spayed or neutered, don't forget to do so.

Prepare a carrier. You want to be prepared to bring your pet home, which means you'll need a carrier. A pet carrier is the finest solution. The hard-sided plastic kind is more durable, but the soft-sided kind will suffice.

Ensure that it is well ventilated. In addition, a hard-sided type will keep your cat safer in the car. If the carrier fits behind the driver's or passenger's seat on the floor, it is the best spot to put it.

Organizing a cat room

One room should be designated as the cat room. Although this area may not always be the cat's, limiting it to one location for a day or longer can help the cat feel safer. Therefore, the cat can consider that its home base to return to once it has ventured out, making it feel more comfortable.

At first, allowing the cat to wander freely may appear to be excessive. Giving it one room allows it to completely investigate that location before going on to the next.

Add a litter box to the mix. This base of operations will require a restroom for your cat. Make sure a litter box is included, as well as litter. Open the crate near the litter box when you first bring your cat in so it knows where it is.

Fill the container with food and water. The cat will, of course, need to eat and drink, so it will need to be in the same room as the litter box. However, try to keep the two separate because most cats don't want to eat and go to the potty in the same location.

Place the litter box and the feeding bowl on separate sides of the room. It is not only preferable for your cat, but it also forces it to explore the entire room.

Add some toys. Toys are a great way to keep a cat occupied, especially if it isn't quite ready to play with you. Jingly balls, scrunchy balls, and mice are all good toys for cats to play with, while string-type toys should be saved for when you can supervise.

Make sure there's somewhere to hide. When they first arrive in a new location, many cats feel the need to conceal. Hiding offers them time to acclimate and gives them a sense of security. As a result, make sure the room you select has adequate hiding places.

A cat tunnel or a cardboard box, for example, can be used as a hiding place. Underneath mattresses (as long as it's free of garbage and grime) and the closet are both ideal options.

Don't forget to bring a sleeping bag. You've placed beds throughout your home, but don't forget to include one in your cat's room as well. It will desire a spot to curl up, but it will most likely construct one for itself if you don't supply one.

A blanket or towel in a cardboard box is ideal for the first few days. It serves as a bed for the cat and a place to hide if it so desires.

Other pets should be kept out. In that vein, keeping them out of the new cat's room for the first day or two is a smart idea. Giving your new cat its place also allows you to gradually introduce the cat to your other pets if you have any. They can get to know one other's odors through the door, allowing them time to acclimate.

Don't just walk away from the cat. The cat room is where you'll get to know your feline companion. Go inside and sit down after the cat has spent a few hours in the room. Talk in a calm tone the entire time and avoid making any unexpected movements. Before the cat approaches, you may need to repeat this process numerous times over several days.

Allow the cat to approach you. Don't bother dragging it out for a snuggle. Allow the cat to sniff you if it approaches. You can also try to pet it softly, although it may flee. It's important to remember that everyone in the house will need to spend some time getting to know the cat. Waving a string toy around will entice the cat to come to play with you, which will help it get to know you.

Chapter Four

RAISING YOUR KITTEN

If you want to raise a cat, be sure you understand the commitment you're making and how to grow it properly. You must provide not only for a cat's most basic needs, such as food and a clean litter box, but also for its health, comfort, and mental well-being. You are more likely to have a well-adjusted, happy, and healthy cat if you do this.

The first contact

New kittens rely on you to keep them safe and healthy in their new surroundings. Here are some things you can do to ensure your kitten's safety and security.

Give them time: a kitten should be adopted at the age of 10 to 12 weeks. Some kittens are adopted as young as six weeks old, although this can be stressful for them and make them scared or shy. A kitten who has been handled carefully by humans will be friendlier and better adjusted, so look for curiosity and confidence in a new cat.

Start with the fundamentals. Young kittens require a safe haven, similar to that they would find if surrounded by their mother and siblings. A blanket-lined cardboard box or a cat bed can serve as a suitable substitute. Kittens require the extra protein and calories found in kitten-formulated diets for the first year, so be sure the food you purchase is specifically designed for them. Place your cat in the box after meals or shortly after waking and gently simulate digging with the kitten's paws to begin litter training. Never reprimand a kitten for not using the litter box properly, and always praise him when he does. To avoid furniture damage, provide a scratching post.

Slowly introduce new family members. Until the kitten adjusts, keep him in a quiet area with a bed, litterbox, and food. Introduce family members one at a time, with children getting additional attention. Teach them how to engage with the kitten carefully, and remind them to wash their hands afterward.

Make your home kitten-proof. Bundle electric cords and keep them out of reach of the kitty. Remove all little items from the room and toxic plants and bug traps. Close the lids on the toilet seat, kitchen cabinets, and washer and dryer lids.

Go through each room one by one. One room at a time, give your kitty the grand tour of the house. Attempt to keep him from hiding behind or under furniture. Simply set him back on the floor when he jumps up or begins the ascent to deter him from jumping on the bed.

Prepare the rest of your creatures. If you already have pets at home, be sure they're in good health before bringing in a new kitten. Give senior cats more attention to help them relax. Allow them to approach the kitten for a few moments to scent each other. Separate them and try again in a few days if they show physical animosity. Don't let your new kitten alone with your dog if you have one. With the dog on a leash, introduce them. Prevent the kitten from running so that the dog does not pursue it. Remember to praise and treat all of your pets for their good conduct during these introductions.

Playtime should be kept safe. Choose toys made specifically for kittens, with no little components that could be swallowed. Tiny stuffed animals or feathers on the end of a small fishing pole are both excellent choices.

First, get a check-up. Make a vet appointment as soon as possible after the kitten arrives, and inform the vet that the cat is new to your home. Making a list of any questions you want to be addressed can be beneficial. Also, ask your veterinarian about spaying and neutering, which can help prevent health problems and overcrowding. Kittens can usually be spayed or neutered at the age of eight weeks, but you and your veterinarian should decide when is the ideal time for your cat.

While you're away, make sure your loved ones are comfortable. Before you leave, put the kitten in a room with a bed, litterbox, scratching post, toys, food, and water. If you are gone all evening, consider adding a nightlight or leaving a light on. You might also try playing music or talk radio for a kitty who is alone—the noises can be relaxing.

Give twice as much affection. Single kittens can be lonely, so consider adopting a pair! If you just have time for one, here's a terrific method to combat loneliness: Wrap a ticking clock in a towel and set it next to his bed; the steady sound reminds him of his mother's heartbeat. Then pick him up and speak to him in a soothing tone to help him relax even more.

Feeding your cat

Provide high-quality cat food. It is critical to provide a cat with nutritional food when raised. Both canned and dried food is acceptable as long as the diet contains primarily animal protein and little filler.

Dry food is better for keeping cats' teeth clean, but it can dehydrate them because cats have a low thirst drive.

If you're not sure what to feed your cat, talk to your veterinarian about it. They'll advise you on what to feed your cat based on its nutritional requirements.

Provide age-appropriate cat food. You should feed your kitten food when it is young, as it has more fat and protein for its developing mind and body. As the cat grows older, you should offer it food that provides sufficient nourishment without causing it to become overweight.

Never change your cat's food all of a sudden. Gradually transition your cat from one food to the next. When your cat reaches a certain age, you may need to switch it to senior food, which has geriatric cats' nutrients.

Give a hairball-preventing cat food to a long-haired cat. Giving your long-haired cat hairball-preventing food is an excellent idea, especially if it has a history of choking on hairballs. This sort of food, in most situations, helps to avoid hairballs by increasing the quantity of fiber your cat consumes. Fiber speeds up digestion and helps food and hair travel more quickly through the digestive tract.

Consult your veterinarian about the best hairball-prevention food for your cat. They might recommend a meal that meets your cat's nutritional needs while also preventing hairballs.

Feed your cat at least twice a day. The amount of food you give it will be determined by its size. Look at the food packaging for portion sizing instructions, usually based on your cat's size and age. Smaller, more frequent meals should be offered to cats who eat too quickly.

Consult your veterinarian about portion sizes and feeding schedules. They may be able to make recommendations based on your cat's individual food requirements to help you keep your cat at a healthy weight. Consult your veterinarian also if your cat is rapidly gaining weight. Obesity in cats can lead to serious health problems such as diabetes and joint pain.

Allow for unrestricted access to drinking water. It's critical to keep clean water on hand for your cat at all times, as dehydration can make your cat extremely unwell. Replace the water in a clean, tiny bowl daily to keep the water pleasant to the cat.

Consider getting a cat drinking fountain. Keep the cat's water away from its food and litter box. The water around these sites is typically seen as contaminated by cats. The recirculating water stream may entice your cat to drink more by attracting its attention.

If your cat exclusively drinks from unattended glasses, leave a separate glass filled with fresh water on the table or counter for your cat! Cats are finicky creatures. If your cat isn't drinking water, it's possible that the water isn't fresh or that the bowl, fountain, or glass is dirty.

Comfort, safety and hygiene

Provide proof of your identity. You should obtain your cat some identification once you've brought it home and given it a name. This can be in the form of a collar tag, or it can be microchipped at its veterinarian's office. Even if you want to keep the cat indoors, identification is necessary because it will have no experience finding its way home if it escapes.

Your cat's name and your phone number should be included on the collar tag. Maintain this phone number so that anyone who finds your cat can simply contact you. Make sure the tags are attached to a collar that has a quick-release buckle. If your cat gets caught on something, the collar will snap off, and the animal will not be harmed.

It's better to have both a collar and a microchip. The collar will allow for easy identification, while the microchip will serve as a backup in the event that the collar is misplaced.

Provide a litter box and demonstrate how to use it. You'll need to train your cat to use a litter box when you're raising it. This is a reasonably simple procedure for most cats. When you first have a cat, keep it in a limited place with food, drink, a bed, and a litter box. Because cats are inherently clean animals who prefer to use specialized bathroom areas, they may naturally go to the litter box to go to the bathroom.

Keep the litter box in a convenient location that is close to your cat's everyday activities. This will make it more likely that the cat will utilize it instead of a convenient area.

If litter box training is proving difficult, keep trying. Move any excrement or urine into the litter box and clean the places where the cat went to the bathroom outside the box if the cat does not use the litter box automatically. If the cat detects excrement and urine in the litter box, it will instinctively go there.

Try a different litter if your cat approaches the litter box but refuses to use it. Your cat may comprehend the importance of using the litter box, but it may dislike the texture of the litter. Cats are intelligent creatures. Consult your veterinarian if your cat continues to refuse to use the litter box; there could be an underlying health issue.

Regularly clean the litter box. You should keep your cat's litter box clean and tidy to guarantee that it is used. Remember to get rid of solids on a daily basis. You should also completely empty it, clean the box, and replace the litter every week. If you don't clean your cat's litter box regularly, it will most likely go to the potty somewhere else.

Make a comfortable sleeping area for your cat. When raising a cat, make sure it has its warm spot to slumber or just relax. This is usually accomplished by providing its own bed and placing it in a peaceful and warm corner. If you live in a busy or congested home, this may be tough to achieve, but your cat may choose the location for itself, and all you have to do is give the cushioning.

Many cats prefer warm, sunny places and have views of the outdoors. Even on frigid days, the sliver of sunlight will suffice to meet your cat's requirements. Some cats prefer to change their napping spots. They may prefer to sleep next to the window one month and nap under the bed the next!

Don't make your cat sleep in a particular area. The cat will become averse to the site and shun it due to this.

Make sure there's a scratching post. Scratching is necessary for all cats to keep their claws healthy and agile. You should get them a scratching post or scratching pad to do this without ruining your furniture. If your cat scratches frequently, you may need to buy or manufacture one for each room.

Place it in front of your cat's favorite scratching location to teach it to use it. Scratch it with your cat's paws, or scratch it yourself! Rub catnip on scratching posts and scratching pads to make them more appealing. Each cat is unique. Try a scratching mat or a cardboard scratching pad if your cat doesn't enjoy scratching posts.

Keep your cat inside the house. If you live in a city, try to train your cat to stay inside. Because they are less likely to contract sickness, be injured, or be abused when they live indoors, they live longer. It also contributes to the safety and well-being of local fauna, such as birds. Provide boxes, cat toys, and sunny window perches for an indoor cat to lounge in for entertainment. You should also consider having at least two cats so that they can entertain each other while you are away.

If you're trying to keep your cat inside, make sure all doors are shut, and all windows and window screens are closed.

Construct a covered patio for your cat. Consider constructing a "catio," which is a cat patio, for your cat to enjoy the sights and fragrances of the outdoors. This is an enclosed outdoor area usually attached to your home and allows your cat to receive some fresh air while not being allowed to roam freely. A catio provides your cat with the stimulation of being outside while also limiting its capacity to become lost or kill wildlife in your neighborhood.

Brush your cat regularly. Depending on the breed, you may need to brush your cat more frequently, but all breeds should be groomed at least once a week. Persian cats, for example, require brushing three to four times a week, whereas American shorthair cats only require brushing once per week. Brushing your cat once a week removes tangles and spare hair that would otherwise rub off on furniture or floors or cause hairballs in your cat.

Cats do not require baths unless they have gotten themselves into something unpleasant and cannot clean themselves. On the other hand, Sphynx cats are hairless and require weekly bathing to keep their skin oils under control.

Keep your cat's claws trimmed. Choose between cat nail clippers, which come in guillotine and scissors styles, or human nail cutters. Place the clippers parallel to the claws. Only the tip of the nail should be trimmed. It is not recommended to cut the quick of nail, which is the back part of the nail with a blood vessel in it.

When your cat is young, start cutting its claws once a week. This will acclimate it to the treatment and make it less resistant as it grows older. Trimming a cat's nails is especially crucial if the cat does not go outside regularly when intense exercise could wear down the nails. Ask a veterinarian or a cat groomer to show you how to clip your cat's claws if you're having problems.

Giving attention and love

Demonstrate your love and affection for your cat. It is critical to show your cat love and affection daily when you are raising them. You can do this by holding it in your lap and petting it every day for a few minutes. This can be accomplished by playing with it and giving it your undivided attention for at least a short time each day. Whatever you do, make sure your cat understands how much you adore it and its importance to your family.

Many cats only require attention on rare occasions and will ask for it when they do. If your cat behaves in this manner, offer it some attention and affection when it asks for it. Your cat's requests may not always come when you expect them, but keep in mind that your cat deserves a little uninterrupted time every day.

Make an effort to socialize your cat. You should start socializing your cat while it is very young if you want to grow a happy and well-adjusted cat. Beginning when your cat is a little kitten, introduce it to a range of individuals so that it understands that this is a regular part of life. Exposing it to a wide range of people and keeping those experiences positive will increase the likelihood that the cat will be friendly and interested in new people and animals as an adult, rather than fearful or hostile.

Exposing your cat to a wide range of sounds and settings is an important part of socialization. When a kitten is exposed to a vacuum cleaner early in life, it is less likely to be afraid of it as an adult.

Provide stimulating toys. Every day, all cats require mental stimulation. This is especially true for kittens whose minds are still forming. This can be achieved in part by providing engaging toys to play with when it is alone. These toys could be motorized cat toys that it chases about or simpler toys like toy mice or balls with bells in them.

You may need to carry many toys home until you find the appropriate one. One by one, try out the toys with your cat until you locate the one it favors. Cats might become bored with toys after playing with them for a long period. Frequently, provide fresh and intriguing toys. Your cat's preferences may alter as they get older. As an adult, a cat who preferred a squeaky mouse toy as a kitten may prefer dangly string.

Interact with your cat regularly. It would help if you spent quality time playing with your cat every day, in addition to offering it toys to play with on its own. It is critical to spend quality interactive time with a cat when raising it to help it develop its brains and personality. Use a feather on a string or a laser pointer to induce the cat to run around and leap into the air. Toss small toys for the cat to pursue, and engage in other cat-friendly activities. This connection is more likely to stimulate the cat than playing alone.

If your cat is very intelligent, you may be able to teach it tricks similar to those taught to dogs.

Veterinary care

Have your cat spayed or neutered. The majority of cats should be spayed or neutered when they are young. The cat will be tamer, and desexing reduces your cat's risk of acquiring diseases such as uterine tumors in female cats. Most vets won't spay or neuter your cat until they're roughly two pounds, so talk to your vet about the best timing.

Another advantage is that you won't have to worry about your female cat going into heat or your male cat spraying indoors and exploring the neighborhood in search of a mate. The only cats that should not be fixed are purebred cats used for breeding by skilled and ethical breeders.

Sterilization is a more expensive option, but it keeps your cat's hormones. You should have both a sterilized male and female cat in this scenario so that they can meet each other's demands. Sterilized cats will still have heat cycles and behave normally, such as roaming (if there is no mate in the house) or spraying (not all full male cats spray).

Bring your cat in for routine veterinary examinations. You must provide regular veterinarian care to a cat to raise it properly. When a cat is young, it usually only requires an annual exam during which the veterinarian analyzes its overall health and administers any necessary vaccines or prescriptions. As your cat gets older, it will most likely require more frequent veterinary visits, usually every six months.

If your cat is typically healthy, veterinary exams may appear to be a waste of money, but they might really save you money in the long term. Early detection of a health problem and treatment can save expenditures as well as your cat's misery and suffering.

Keep your preventative medication up to date. Discuss flea medicines and immunizations with your veterinarian when you bring your cat in for a check-up. They would most likely recommend a frequent flea repellent treatment, such as Frontline or Trifexis, that you can administer at home if you have fleas. It is critical to keep up with this treatment to avoid a flea infestation in your cat.

Follow your veterinarian's recommendations for immunizations and boosters. They'll offer recommendations based on your cat's exposure risk and medical history. Vaccinations for panleukopenia, herpesvirus, calicivirus, rabies, feline leukemia, chlamydiosis, infectious peritonitis, immunodeficiency, bordetella, and giardiasis may be recommended by the veterinarian.

Chapter Five

BASIC CAT TRAINING

Dare I claim that cats are just as much fun to train as dogs? Your cat will enjoy learning simple commands, and most kittens will respond well to leash training, provided the lessons are accompanied by food and entertainment. If done correctly, with patience and rewards, many cats enjoy training. You receive out what you put in, just like in any other relationship!

While cats cannot be educated to perform the wide range of duties dogs are bred, they have a natural aptitude for basic training. Cats will use a litter box naturally, and common dog behavior issues such as play biting, separation anxiety, and hostility are simple to avoid.

Training a cat not to do anything, such as bite or pull on a leash, frequently boils down to not triggering the action in the first place. If you're leash training, use a harness rather than a training collar, which might cause a frantic oppositional response and cause your cat to choke. If your cat bites, redirect their predatory instincts to a feathery toy and educate them what to do instead.

Cat training has numerous advantages. Mental and physical stimulation, as well as pleasant social interaction, are all provided by training. Just the act of training is quite beneficial for disgruntled, bored, shy, and fearful cats.

Before you begin cat training, take a minute to stroll around in her paws. Cats are more like teens than dogs, interacting with their families like toddlers. Cats are motivated on a pay-to-play basis, whereas dogs would cooperate in exchange for a few sweet words. Despite our gushing enthusiasm, Cats will only participate in training games if the benefits are worthwhile.

Seven tricks you can teach your cat

Cat training is an excellent method to bond with your cat while also teaching them the meaning of a few essential phrases. The most important thing is to give your cat an ultimate choice over what you teach them; not all cats enjoy doing everything. Before attempting to train your cat to perform a behavior on command, choose actions that come easily to your cat.

Maintain an optimistic attitude. Clicker training is a great technique to pinpoint exactly when your cat performs the behavior you're looking for. In a nutshell, training is nothing more than associating words with natural activities and rewarding your cat for participating. Here are seven words and acts that your cat should learn:

1. Be gentle.

Encourage your cats to perceive hands as a constant source of pleasure. As your cat or kitten licks your hand, say "gentle," and pull your hand away calmly if they start to pinch or bite. Dab a little homemade or store-bought treat paste on your knuckles or the back of your hand to avoid biting.

2. Locate It

Yes, it's that straightforward. Toss high-value goodies at your cat's paws and add the word "Find It" once your cat can follow the toss. The shell game can then be played with Tupperware containers or your hands. If she claws or bites your hand, say "gentle" and use a dab of cat paste to encourage licking. After she licks or taps your palm lightly with her paw, reveal the treat.

3. Set a goal

A man-made or store-bought target wand, or even the tip of your finger, can be used. Present the target 2 inches in front of your cat's nose to teach them to be aware of it. Click and reward them as soon as they touch it. Say the word "target" to put this behavior on cue once your cat reliably moves to the target.

4. Take a seat

Click and treat your cat whenever she sits naturally. When you put out the treats, you'll notice your cat sitting to cue you. Once you've figured out what she'll do, add the phrase "sit." Then use a target wand or a pointing signal to entice her into place. This stance should be rewarded with a click. Gradually stop clicking every correct response and only use the clicker and goodies when necessary.

5. Stay on your mat

Lay a flat mat, towel, or cloth napkin on the counter, sofa, or tabletop to make a cat-mat. Curiosity won't kill your cat, but it will give her the upper hand! Click when she steps on the cat-mat. Then toss a reward a few inches away from the mat, forcing your cat to return for the next round. Gradually incorporate "on your mat" as a cue. Introduce the "stay" cue if your cat is willing to go to her mat and stay there. While you eat or cook, use the cat-mat to encourage your cat to stay in a specific spot, such as her cat tree. You may also take your cat-mat on vacation or to the veterinarian to calm your cat during appointments.

6. Please come.

From the moment they enter your home, cats can learn to come. Combine happy memories with the sound of a treat cup being shaken with the word "coming." To accomplish this, place treats in a cup or container, shake it, and reward your cat until they recognize the sound. When your cat arrives, click and give her a treat. Gradually shorten the time between saying "come" and shaking the rewards until she responds on cue. Gradually remove the clicker and treat her regularly.

7. Outside the Box (or Cat Carrier)

The majority of cats will readily leap into a box or investigate a bag. Having a direction for this action is helpful when it's time to draw out the cat carrier. Pull out the cat carrier before you need it, hide treats inside, and even feed your cat or kitten portions of her meal in it. Click and reward your cat when he jumps into the carrier or a box. Add the cue "in the box" when your cat prompts you. Gradually increase the amount of time you spend carrying her around in her box/carrier, praising her after each ride.

Because lessons typically need strong concentration, keep them short and upbeat. End each one with a predatory game, including a feather flyer or a stuffed toy, which you should let your cat carry away in victory.

Don'ts in cat training

Discipline has little effect on cats, and they do not learn from it. Swatting, spraying, or frightening your cat may stop them from doing a specific behavior around you, but they will not stop the habit in general. Your presence will be a buzzkill, causing a suspicious cat to be apprehensive of your proximity.

Cats communicate through their actions, especially the ones we don't like. Any punitive strategy or aimed to reduce a behavior just prevents dialogue from taking place. Rather than focusing on what you don't want, focus your training on what you do want.

Things to remember during training

As we learned, cats are intelligent and trainable creatures! You can teach them a lot if you find the perfect technique to work with them. Your cat will become more social, less worried, and more content due to training. Below are some essential points that we must never forget.

1. What do you want your cat to learn from you?

First and foremost, think about what you want your cat to learn. Do you want to teach your cat some fun tricks (like high fives) or prevent undesirable behavior (like furniture scratching)? The strategy you use will be dictated by the type of behavior you want to teach. Once you've determined what you want to work on, you may begin steadily moving forward with your pet. The following are some of the most typical goals in cat training:

- Making use of the litter box
- There will be no scratching or leaping on the furniture.
- There will be no biting
- Come, sit, stay, high five, roll over, jump, and other orders are followed.
- Getting a cat to stop doing something
- It's possible to teach a cat new tricks.

2. Keep cat training sessions to a minimum.

A lesson's length and duration must be tailored to your cat's mood and interest. Cats have a shorter attention span than humans and like to do things their way and at their own pace. This means you'll have to train your pet whenever they're interested and for as long as they're interested. Short, frequent, and natural training sessions are frequently the most successful. It's critical to stay cool, patient, and, most importantly, persistent. Don't give up if your cat isn't progressing as quickly as you'd like. They are self-reliant and determined, which necessitates a lot of patience on your part.

3. Concentrate on a single behavior action at a time.

While cats may learn multiple things at once, it is assumed that teaching them one thing at a time is the most effective method. Allow your cat to master the current objective before moving on to the next one for the best results.

4. Rewarding positive behavior with effective cat training

Positive reinforcement works really well with cats. Our beloved pets like performing things that benefit them in some way. As a result, if your feline does something good, praise her, scratch her, or give her a treat. You can also use the "clicker" to reward them each time. They'll be able to relate the goal, the reward, and the clicker sound in this way. They'll know they performed a good job every time they hear the clicker.

5. Do not reprimand negative behavior.

Cats are notoriously bad at taking punishment. This type of disciplinary approach is not effective, and it frequently causes stress and anxiety. Instead, attempt to distract your cat if you notice unacceptable behavior. For example, if you're training them not to scratch the furniture, make a fast, harsh sound (i.e., "whoa!") every time you see them do it. The cat will become preoccupied, and the action will come to a halt. Avoid using common words like "hey" or "no," and keep your sound choices consistent. This will prevent them from becoming perplexed when they hear these sounds in other circumstances.

6. Involve other people

Other family members and frequent visitors should be included in your training as well. Everyone should be aware of the final goal and the means you're using to achieve it. Every individual who sees the cat scratching the sofa, for example, must react and take the same corrective action as you.

7. Get started right away.

If you're taking a kitten home, you should start teaching them particular behaviors as soon as possible. Socializing kittens and acclimating them to being handled and groomed, for example, is much easier while they are young. This kind of kitten raising will make it easier for us to care for them as they get older.

Identifying and correcting unacceptable behavior

Many of us would rather start with the fundamentals before moving on to the more advanced techniques. We'd prefer our cats to utilize their litter boxes and refrain from mischief like biting, scratching furniture, or climbing on counters.

1. The first step is getting the cat to use the litter box.

The first step in this quest is to locate a suitable litter box location. It should be conveniently accessible and located in a calm, secluded location that is not too far away. Above all, keep the litter box clean and fresh at all times.

You can begin training your cat after the litter box has been installed. Shortly after the cat has eaten, place them in the litter box and gently scratch the sand with their front paw until they urinate. This should be done multiple times. Your cat should quickly figure out what the litter box is for.

You'll want to praise and thank your kitty just after they've done eating at first. However, do not reprimand them for littering outside of the litter box. They won't learn anything from it, and you might even make them anxious or afraid.

2. Getting the cat to stop biting

It's critical to understand when and why your cat bites in the first place for this task. Is it a rough player, or does it lash out when you infringe on their personal space? If your cat starts biting and clawing you during a game, you should down the game as soon as they become too violent. Disengage from the activity and ignore your pet by standing or sitting still. If you stick to this strategy, they'll figure out that you won't play with them if they're too rough. If they attack you because you are handling them too much for their liking, simply respect their boundaries.

If a cat isn't receiving enough exercise, it may become aggressive. You can help them by offering more opportunities to express their predatory impulses. Provide them with a variety of toys to flick, chase, and catch. Some toys, such as "fishing" toys, let you participate in the hunting game alongside your pet.

3. Teach your cat not to scratch your furniture.

If your cat is scratching the furniture, they may simply require scratching. Provide a scratching post for them to use to sharpen their claws. Distract your cat with a startling, unusual sound anytime you notice undesirable conduct. It will make them aware of the situation, but it will not cause them to panic. Make an effort to use the same sound each time.

However, do not declaw your cat. This will not address the problem and may even exacerbate it.

Cat training techniques to try

1. Arrive when summoned

Howcast, a YouTube user, created a fantastic video on How to Train a Cat to Come When Called. They recommend shouting your cat's name while holding a bag of their favorite treats. When they come to you, you should reward them. They'll soon realize the link between their name and the delectable prize. Once they've progressed, you can start substituting compliments and encouraging head scratches for the treats.

2. Take a seat

If you're training your cat to sit, you might want to use a hand signal in addition to the vocal instruction. With your treat and clicker in hand, stand in front of your cat and say "sit" in a calm, steady voice while holding your palm vertically in a stop sign. When your cat sits down while you're doing this, give them a treat and click the clicker.

3. Give yourself a high five

It's a lot easier than it appears to teach your cat to give you a high five. Begin encouraging their paw motions while also treating them whenever their paw leaves the ground. Then, wrap the goodie in your fist and wait for their paw to try to grasp it. Reward them when they accomplish this. Lift your hand higher and higher as you progress. Reward them every time they contact your hand with their paw. As you train them, don't forget to utilize the vocal command and say "hive five" or "shake paw." Your cat will quickly learn that they should give you a high five whenever you extend your hand and say the magic word!

Chapter Six

UNDERSTANDING CAT BEHAVIORS

Cats have some common behaviors that may appear bizarre to the eyes of the unfamiliar. In this chapter, I will analyze some of them and try to explain their origins and how to manage them.

Why do cats love boxes?

Cats are known for their fondness for boxes. Most cat enthusiasts have seen at least one cartoon depicting a cat napping in a box rather than the costly cat bed inside the box. Why are cats so fond of boxes? The reasons can be numerous, but the bottom line is that it provides a safe and comfortable place for your cat to rest.

Cats' perceptions of boxes

Cats are naturally curious creatures. When something new appears in their environment, they check to see whether it is safe, if it is a toy, or if it could be food. Cats are predators by nature. A box is a limited, enclosed location that your cat can consider as the ideal place to hide and ambush prey.

Some people overlook the fact that, while cats are predators, they are also prey for various wild creatures. An enclosed box can also serve as a secure haven for your cat. In fact, boxes may make your cat feel so safe that they choose to hide inside one when they are stressed or when the environment in their house changes. Hiding is a coping mechanism for cats who are exposed to a variety of stressors in their surroundings.

Some cat owners might ask why, if the cat carrier is a confined place that resembles a box, the cat despises it so much. Regrettably, your cat has figured out what the carrier signifies. When they're at home, putting their belongings in the carrier signifies they're going somewhere unpleasant, like the vet. This is also why your cat only wants to go back into the carrier while you're at the vet. When they get in the carrier at the vet, it signifies they're heading home. However, certain techniques help you get your cat into their carrier. If you start early, leaving the carrier out as an extra bed (or box) will help break your cat's relationship with it and the vet.

The enchantment of boxes

The texture is everything to cats. This may explain why switching diets for a cat who has only eaten a specific kibble shape can be problematic and why canned food textures vary. Your cat may prefer scratching at your couch over the sisal rope scratching post set up right next to it due to texture preferences. Most cats will like scratching and nibbling on cardboard because of its texture.

Cardboard also acts as an insulator. Temperatures in the upper 80s to lower 90s are ideal for cats (in Fahrenheit). This is certainly warmer than most people's thermostat settings. Cardboard crates could provide a comfortable haven for your cat.

How to promote positive box experiences

There are several things you can do to keep your cat safe and comfortable if they insist on sleeping in boxes. Fill the box with soft blankets and several of your cat's favorite toys. To help them feel even more at ease, spritz their bedding with a relaxing pheromone like Feliway. Cats want to be near their owners, so place the box in a common part of the house, such as the family room or the bedroom.

Safety suggestions

Before you give your cat a cardboard box to play with, keep the following in mind:

- Remove any staples that may have been embedded in the cardboard. These could accidentally poke your cat or puncture a wound that could become infectious.
- Remove any twine or string used to close the box because these can cause a linear foreign body in cats.
- Place the box on a stable surface, such as the floor, on its largest side to prevent it from tipping over.
- If you're packing boxes for a move, make sure your cat hasn't gotten into one before you close it.

For the most part, cats' preoccupation with boxes is a perfectly natural behavior. Don't be afraid to embrace it. They'll eventually notice the pricey toy or pet bed that came with it.

Why do cats meow at night?

Cats aren't as loud as dogs, but that doesn't mean they don't express themselves. Cats make meows, screams, yowls, cries, and other noises. These noises can occur during the day as a result of many stimuli, but they are more common at night while you are trying to sleep.

Why isn't your cat getting enough sleep?

Cats are naturally active and awake at night, which is inconvenient for you. They may want to play, explore, eat, itch, or attract your attention, and their activity can be extremely loud, causing us to wake up. During the day, some cats are extremely lazy. Because they didn't use much energy while you were awake, these cats will have a lot of energy to burn at night.

At night, I'm meowing for attention

If your cat is lively, curious, and enjoys playing, their meows may be waking you up in the middle of the night. Cats will scratch at your bedroom door, paw at you, bump into you, flop down on the floor in front of you, and, of course, meow to seek your attention. If your cat is calling for your attention while you're sleeping, the best thing you can do right now is ignore them. This is understandably difficult for some people, but if you pay attention to your cat while they are meowing for it, you will just be reinforcing the unpleasant habit. Even if you yell at your cat and give it bad attention, you are still giving it attention. Earplugs may be your only option until you figure out how to stop the nighttime meowing.

The next day, make sure you're wearing your cat out by giving it toys to play with during the day. Toys like puzzles, feather wands, laser pointers, and battery-operated chase toys are excellent options. Some pet cameras even have laser pointers that you can operate while you're at work, allowing you to interact with your cat even while you're not at home. Your cat will be less likely to meow at night if you tire it and give it all the attention it needs during the day.

At night, I'm meowing for food

Have you neglected to feed your cat? Cats frequently call for food or treats, and a hungry cat in the middle of the night is not a peaceful cat. If your cat is hungry, you won't get much sleep, so feed it before going to bed. Do not get up in response to your cat's cries in the middle of the night since this will just teach your cat that if it meows at you, you will feed it. Consider an automatic cat feeder if you have a busy work schedule or are worried about forgetting to feed your cat. It allows you to set the mealtime and amount of food your cat will receive. This will ensure a consistent feeding schedule, and your cat will be less inclined to associate you with food. Make sure your cat has access to fresh water at all times to avoid thirst as a cause of nightly activity and noise.

Because of cognitive dysfunction, I'm meowing

Like people with dementia, Cats can acquire cognitive impairment that makes it difficult for them to understand what's going on around them. It's not completely understood in cats, but we do know that elderly cats who seem disoriented and meow for no apparent reason tend to get worse at night.

If you feel your cat is suffering from cognitive dysfunction, consult your veterinarian for a definitive diagnosis and treatment options. Special meals and nutritional supplements may be prescribed to maintain your cat's brain operating as well as possible.

Anxiety, Stress, Discomfort, and Pain Cause Meowing

Any health condition or event that causes anxiety, stress, discomfort, or pain in your pet might cause them to become agitated and noisy.

If your cat exhibits daytime or nighttime behavioral changes or physical symptoms of sickness, consult your veterinarian.

Meowing due to vision problems or deafness

A cat that can't see or hear well may be terrified or perplexed. Your home is usually darker and quieter at night than during the day, and if your cat's vision is fading or they are deaf and can't see you, they may meow for assistance or comfort. Because they can't hear themselves well, your cat may be unaware that they're meowing loudly. Eyesight and hearing can decrease with age and disease, so consult your veterinarian if your previously well-sighted and hearing-capable cat appears to be losing its senses.

Why cats chase lasers

The never-ending battle between cat and laser pointer is well-known among cat parents. That little red dot, despite (or perhaps because of) the fact that it is so little and scentless, can certainly keep cats occupied. However, there is still disagreement as to whether laser pointers are a good toy for our feline companions. So, why do cats chase lasers, and is it time to switch to a different toy?

Laser's Allure

Because of what they represent: fast-moving prey, lasers are naturally stimulating to cats. It doesn't mean your cat isn't hardwired for the job just because it doesn't have to work for it (unless you count the effort it takes to meow all morning until you fill up its dish).

Your cat sees a little animal trying to flee and hide as a laser dot darts about the room. It doesn't matter that it's only a projection because your cat is on auto-pilot, not thinking. As a result, certain natural feline instincts emerge, most notably the drive to hunt, pounce, and kill the prey.

Laser vision in cats

When your cat follows a laser, there's also the matter of how tempting it looks. It helps to understand how your cat's eyes work and how they differ from human eyes to comprehend why.

One of the most important parts of the eye is the retina. Rods and cones are the two main cell types. Cones help the eye see color while rods deal with low light vision and detecting movement. Because human eyes have more cones than rods, we see a lot of color in the world. On the other hand, Cats have more rods than cones, allowing them to detect even the tiniest movement.

What's the connection between this and lasers? This means they're difficult to overlook. Your cat will pick up a laser point in its peripheral vision the instant you turn it on, and if it hasn't yet figured out that it can't actually eat that red dot (or if it knows it can but doesn't care), that will be all it takes for it to begin its predatory cycle.

Cats vs. Lasers

It may come as a surprise to learn that there is a discussion about whether or not it is a good idea to tempt your cat with lasers, but the cat-laser argument has been raging for quite some time.

According to anti-laser cat aficionados, having your cat chase a laser is a sort of taunting. Remember that your cat is chasing and pouncing on the red dot because its brain tells it to catch and kill the food. Even if the cat is having a good time, it's not doing it as a sort of play.

The laser is an unreachable target, and no matter how good your cat's hunting abilities are, it will never be able to consume it and complete its predatory cycle. Many cats become aware of the hoax and cease interacting with the laser. Others may become irritated as a result and begin misbehaving. Cats who are frustrated behave out in less than ideal ways, such as being destructive or aggressive. It's probably time to put the pointer away for good if you see a link between playing with your cat with a laser and negative behavior.

Give your cat a treat or a tangible toy right after you stop playing with laser pointers to help make it more of a game and less of a tease. That way, even if it's not the laser, it'll have the satisfaction of a "kill."

Safe use of a laser pointer

There's probably nothing to be concerned about if your cat appears to like chasing a laser and isn't stuck in a never-ending cycle of hunt-pounce-disappointment. Chasing a laser is an excellent way for your cat to get some physical and mental activity while also allowing it to indulge in its natural kitty instincts—something that indoor cats don't get to do nearly as often as they'd like.

Of course, you must observe all safety precautions to keep your cat safe when playing. Here are two noteworthy examples.

Keep the light away from your cat's eyes. Even toy lasers create an astonishing amount of light, so don't aim it at your cat (or yourself!). You risk causing vision issues and/or eye damage if you do so.

Other toys should be available for your cat. It's more likely that your cat will become frustrated if the laser is their only source of entertainment. Make sure it has access to various other items, including catnip toys and wands, for hunting and playing.

Why cats dislike water

Water isn't something that all cats despise. Cats who have had pleasant experiences near and in water, particularly during their important socialization stage (early socialization happens between 3 and 8 weeks, late socialization occurs between 9 and 16 weeks), are more likely to enjoy it. Some breeds enjoy being in the water! It's critical to approach your cat as an individual with no preconceived notions.

Many cats have developed a dislike towards the water.

Cats are said to have been domesticated in the Middle East 9,500 years ago. They originated in arid desert environments without access to rivers, lakes, or rain. As a result, cats nowadays tend to avoid sources of water. Rain and thunderstorms cause even community cats to seek cover. In today's cats, avoiding water has become instinctive.

This isn't true for all breeds, as some cats prefer to be in the water because of their evolutionary history. The Turkish Van and Turkish Angora, for example, are recognized for their affinity for water and ability to swim. They adapted to their climate by shedding their hair in the summer to swim and fish in the Lake Van region of Turkey. Bengals, Maine Coons, and American Bobtails are other breeds that appreciate water.

Scent sensitivity in cats

Cats have a sense of smell that is fourteen times more sensitive than ours. The strong aromas included in shampoos and conditioners may contribute to cats' dislike of water and bathing. Some people believe that your cat dislikes the smell of pollutants in tap water.

Cats enjoy being clean and warm

Cats are naturally clean creatures who spend a significant amount of time grooming themselves by keeping their fur clean, detangled, and well-conditioned. Cats also have a greater body temperature and washing themselves aids in maintaining and regulating it. When a cat's coat gets wet, it becomes rather thick, making it difficult for them to rapidly go back to a dry, warm state. A wet coat might also make the cat seem slower and less nimble than usual, giving the unpleasant sense of being unable to rapidly escape a situation.

Water intolerance

Many cats' experiences with water have been negative—being trapped in a downpour without shelter, being sprayed with water, and being made to bathe are just a few examples—so it's logical that they dislike it.

Do cats require bathing?

Cats, as previously said, do an excellent job of keeping themselves clean and can spend up to 40% of their day doing it, so you may never need to bathe your cat.

Senior, arthritic, and overweight cats may have difficulty accessing particular portions of their bodies, necessitating a medical bath. If the cat has rolled in something sticky or unpleasant, a bath may be required.

How can I make my cat like baths?

- Before Taking a Bath

Allow yourself to become accustomed to the surroundings. Try acclimating your cat to the tub weeks before a bath to help her become used to the environment. Fill an empty tub or sink with toys, catnip, or goodies to help your cat form positive associations with the space. Spread spreadable delicacies on the tub for your cats to lick, such as a little quantity of squeeze cheese, whip cream, or anchovy paste.

Fill the tub with an inch or two of warm water and spread toys throughout it so your cat may have some fun with it after she's comfortable playing and eating goodies in the sink or tub. Encourage your cat to play with the toys by praising her and rewarding her with treats.

Before bathing the cat, make sure you have everything you need. Make sure you have everything you'll need. This contains cat-specific shampoo, favorite snacks and toys, warm towels, a plastic cup for pouring water over your cat, a non-slip surface, such as a rubber liner, and a bath mat or towel for your cat to stand on in the sink or bathtub.

Create a relaxing atmosphere. Keep noises to a minimum by closing the door. Maintain a cool demeanor and speak quietly. If your spray attachment makes a lot of noise, try rinsing your cat with a couple of cups of water instead. If you're stressed, so will your cat!

- Throughout the bath

Use positive distractions and minimum restraint. Scuffing and squeezing your cat is not a good idea. Instead, use gentleness, pay attention to your cat's body language, and provide positive distractions such as a unique spreadable treat and/or a wand toy.

Take special precautions to avoid spraying your face or getting water in your ears or eyes. It's best not to wash your whiskers. Many of a cat's touch receptors are located in its whiskers; therefore, it's only logical that cats dislike having these receptors grazed by water, food, or dirt. To avoid skin sensitivity, properly rinse the shampoo.

- Following the bath

Dry with a towel. Gently remove your cat out of the water and wrap it in a warm towel to dry; alternatively, if your cat prefers not to be carried, allow the water to drain and towel dry while still in the tub. Finish with a cat snuggle or a game of fetch, as well as your cat's favorite treat! Your cat will dry spontaneously in a few hours, so keep them warm and away from drafts during that time.

Why cats (sometimes) eat litter

For various reasons, cats will eat litter and other unwanted stuff. Pica, or the eating of non-food objects, is the term for this activity.

Pica can have a multitude of causes, including a mother leaving her kittens, which can result in nursing behavior. Pica-affected cats can eat anything, including plastic, fabric, twine, paper, dirt, and even litter. Pica can be harmless or bothersome in some cases, such as licking plastic bags, but consuming non-food things can create intestinal obstructions. It might also be a symptom of a disease.

Cats eat litter for several reasons

It could be a health or behavior concern if your cat or kitten eats litter. If you suspect a health problem, take your cat to the doctor as soon as possible, especially if the behavior occurs unexpectedly. Some kittens may consume litter out of curiosity, but they will grow out of the habit with close supervision.

- Anemia

Eating litter could indicate that your cat is ill, and anemia is one illness that can cause this behavior. Anemia is defined as a shortage of red blood cells and hemoglobin in the body. Cat owners should check Gums that are pale, white, or bluish. A lack of iron, trace minerals, vitamins, or vital fatty acids can cause anemia.

Additionally, if your cat is eating litter, it could indicate leukemia or kidney problems (both of which induce anemia). Your veterinarian will perform a complete blood count (CBC) and urinalysis as part of a normal exam. The blood count will disclose whether or not the cat has anemia, and the urinalysis will reveal the urine's concentration level; excessively dilute pee indicates kidney disease. Your veterinarian will take radiographs or an MRI if your cat exhibits symptoms of blockage.

- Deficiencies in vitamins and minerals

If your cat isn't getting enough nourishment from its food, it may be eating litter. Vitamin A, Vitamin B1 (Thiamine), L-Carnitine, Magnesium, Pyruvate Kinase, Sodium, and/or Taurine deficiency in cats can also cause litter eating. Minerals in the clay-based litter may help to compensate for the deficit. Your veterinarian or a veterinary nutritionist may recommend dietary adjustments or supplements.

- Curiosity

Kittens may eat litter out of curiosity, it's best to wait until they're older before using clumping litter. When you eat clumping litter, you risk getting an intestinal blockage. Use a non-toxic litter and keep an eye on it. If you notice your kitten eating the litter, take it out of the box—but only after it has finished its business.

Adult cats may eat litter if the type of litter has recently been changed, such as to wheat- or corn-based litter.

What to do when it happens

You can focus on changing your cat's behavior away from eating the litter once he's been given a clean bill of health. Of course, litter comes in a variety of forms, including clay, clumping (smelling and unscented), corn, wheat, and paper. If your cat only eats one type, try a different one.

- It's possible that your cat is bored. To entice him away from the box, toss a crinkle ball or a toy mouse, or dangle a fishing pole toy. Redirect the behavior with play if you find it eating litter.

- Rethink your cat's eating habits. Upgrade your pet's food, particularly if it's supermarket-grade dry food. Nutritionally, many high-quality food selections are more complete.

- Enhance your cat's natural hunting instincts. Look at food puzzle toys, which foster natural foraging behavior, in addition to increasing playtime. There are numerous various versions available in pet stores and many ways to make your own from common household objects. Puzzle toys provide a pleasant method for your cat to work for its food while diverting its attention away from unwanted behavior.

- Try giving your cat a pot of cat grass. This serves as a distraction from the litter box and provides your cat with something to gnaw on. Don't forget about catnip, the perennial favorite of joyful cats. Grow your own and serve it fresh, sprinkle it on scratchers, or purchase catnip-filled toys.

Why cats knock things over

Cats are known for knocking items off counters and shelves. In fact, a fast internet search will turn up a slew of videos and comics about cats smashing objects by doing just that. Any cat owner will find this aggravating. Why do cats insist on destroying our trinkets? There are various reasons why your cat enjoys knocking things over, as with most pet activities.

Instincts of predation

Cats, especially those kept indoors, have solid predatory instincts. This is due to the fact that they are "real" carnivores. Cat toys like wand toys, laser pointers, and kick sticks are entertaining for your cat because they allow them to express their natural tendencies. They're attempting to figure out if your pen is possible prey by knocking it about your desk. Cats will explore their surroundings not just with their noses but also with their paws. As a result, even things that don't resemble a mouse or bug may receive a cursory nudge from your cat.

Boredom

Cats are incredibly intelligent, far more so than many people believe. Cats can quickly become bored if they aren't provided enough cerebral stimulation. Many seeming "non-necessary" habits can originate merely as a result of your cat's demand for additional stimulation. If your cat isn't getting enough excitement from active play, he may begin ripping up your furniture, climbing your curtains, and playing with items that aren't designed to be cat toys, such as items left on counters.

Search of attention

After a few occasions knocking something off a counter, a cat learns that when they knock something over, their owner comes racing. If your cat is trying to grab your attention, they may start knocking objects off counters. If your cat knocks something over, try not to run over it right away to avoid reinforcing the behavior. Obviously, make sure your cat doesn't get hurt if they smash a coffee mug or knock over a container of food, but dropped pens and keys may be picked up later.

What can you do to stop this from happening again?

It's not a good idea to chastise your cat for knocking things over because this is a natural tendency. However, there are a few things you can do to reduce the amount of damage your cat causes by knocking objects off counters. Scheduled play periods, particularly with toys that appeal to predatory tendencies, such as wand toys and kick sticks, can help keep boredom at bay. These toys give mental and physical stimulation as well as an acceptable outlet for your cat's instincts. Playing with your cat regularly will help them lose their fascination with knocking objects off counters. It's critical, though, that this playtime lasts more than a few minutes. Every day, most cats will benefit from 20 minutes of active play. Redirection, in addition to regular playtime, can be beneficial. If you notice your cat about to leap onto a counter or table containing items they might like to knock over, you can divert their attention with an impromptu play session.

Toy rotation is another strategy to keep your cat interested in their toys rather than your stray pens. It's critical to provide your cat with a range of toys to play with, but it's also critical to rotate those toys so they don't become bored. Simply store half of your cat's toys in a plastic storage tote with some dry catnip sprinkled on top to rotate them. Collect all of the toys that are out and replace them with the toys in the storage tote once a week.

Finally, puzzle feeders are a useful item to have on hand. If your cat is already kicking items off your counters, puzzle feeders, particularly those that get pushed around, so the kibble falls out, can be a nice outlet for them. You can also reduce their desire to knock objects over by restricting their access to them. If you want to keep curiosities on display, put them in an enclosed curio cabinet or on high shelves out of reach of your cat.

You can't stop your cat from pawing at objects out of habit. You may give them proper outlets for this behavior if you understand why they feel compelled to do so.

Why cats lick themselves so often

Cats are preferred by many pet owners over dogs because "cats are so clean." And it's true: a typical cat can spend up to half of their awake hours grooming themselves (or another cat). As a result, cats are normally highly clean creatures, albeit grooming can become an obsession in some situations.

<u>Starting with a clean slate</u>

After giving birth, the mother cat's first function is to remove the amniotic sac and then kiss the kitten with her rough tongue to help it breathe. She will then give the kitten's anus a "tongue massage" to help encourage a bowel movement once the kitten begins nursing.

By the time they're a few weeks old, kittens imitate their mothers and groom themselves. If they're in a litter, they'll probably lick and groom each other as well.

Grooming serves a variety of benefits beyond plain cleanliness. Here are a few of the most crucial.

To Get rid of injuries

Cats clean their wounds to keep them clean and potentially prevent infection. Dead skin cells can also be removed by licking with a hard tongue.

To protect your scent from predators

The sense of smell in cats is fourteen times stronger than in humans. The scent is used by most predators, including cats, to track prey. In the wild, a mother cat would try to conceal her small kittens by obliterating evidence of their feeding. After nursing, she will properly wash and them. Cats will bury uneaten dead prey in the wild for the same reason. When you see a cat clawing at the floor surrounding the food dish after it has eaten, you may notice the same natural behavior.

Coat and skin grooming and lubrication

Cats groom by stimulating the sebaceous glands at the base of their hairs and spreading the resulting oil throughout the hairs with their barb-like tongues. Self-grooming also aids in the removal of dirt and parasites such as fleas from the coat. Furthermore, because cats lack sweat glands, their saliva assists them in cooling off on hot days.

For the sake of pleasure

Grooming is pleasurable, and cats appear to groom simply for the pleasure of it. They will also groom one another (and their human companions) out of what appears to be a desire to share a pleasurable experience.

<u>When cat grooming turns into an obsession</u>

Excessive grooming can develop an obsessive-compulsive disorder, resulting in bald patches and skin ulcers.

Over-grooming in cats is generally a result of stress, and it's similar to people biting their nails quickly. Cats, on the whole, despise change of any type. This excessive grooming could be triggered by a new birth, a death in the family, or even furniture shifting. Flea bites or ringworm are examples of physical causes; thus, these must be ruled out before diagnosing a stress response.

Cats who were separated from their moms at a young age were not permitted to go through the usual weaning process and often groom themselves by licking or sucking. This tendency will normally reduce and disappear with time when the kitten is kept in a safe and predictable setting.

Why cats act crazy

Does your cat have a nocturnal burst of energy, complete with a chorus of meows, and suddenly race around the house? This "crazy" behavior in cats may catch you off guard, and a cat's body language is far more difficult to decipher than that of a dog. If you've ever wondered why your cat suddenly becomes crazy, strange, or zany, there are a few plausible explanations.

Every cat, regardless of breed, has moments when they dash across a room, meow like crazy, and act as if they're being followed on a racetrack. They dart about quicker and faster, gazing all over the place, before coming to a halt.

Your cat could try to entice you to participate in the fun by jumping on your bed and pawing at your feet, elbows, hair, or face. When this type of activity occurs at night, it is commonly referred to as "midnight crazies." the reasons for this erratic and occasionally humorous conduct are several.

Instinct for predation

Domestic cats retain this impulse to some extent because they are natural predators. A cat acting erratically could be displaying hunting skills, combat movements, or escape techniques.

Even though a house cat doesn't have to search for food, it still has to expend pent-up energy, which may manifest itself as bizarre behavior. Catnip mice, laser pointers, food puzzles, and feather wands are examples of toys that stimulate a cat to use its natural tendencies to grab, chase, and jump. If your cat doesn't get enough exercise outside, this is very crucial.

Instincts of the night

Another reason for your cat's strange behavior could be because some cats are nocturnal, which means they are more active at night. A cat that doesn't get enough exercise during the day may act erratically.

While their owners are at work, many domestic cats spend their days alone indoors. When the cat's owner returns home in the evening, the cat is likely to be highly active and eager to play. The cat may act crazily if it doesn't have a way to release all of its pent-up energy. Kittens are particularly active.

Senility

If you have an elderly cat, it's likely acting strangely due to senility or cognitive problems. As a pet gets older, its brain may begin to work differently, resulting in unusual behavior for no apparent reason.

Fleas

Because it has fleas, a cat may act erratically and appear as if something is biting it. Your cat may be hypersensitive to flea bites or simply have an itch it can't reach, especially when meowing is involved.

If you suspect your cat has fleas, treat all of the household's furry members with a prescription flea-killing and prevention treatment formulated exclusively for cats. You should also contact your veterinarian to examine whether the fleas have caused any secondary skin illnesses or allergies that need to be addressed. You'll also need to treat the environment by vacuuming, doing laundry, and using flea bombs or area sprays if your veterinarian recommends it. Your cat should cease acting like this after the fleas are gone.

Feline Hyperesthesia Syndrome (FHS)

Feline hyperesthesia syndrome (FHS) is a rare reason for a cat to act erratically, affecting mostly older cats and with no recognized cause. If you see any of the following, talk to your veterinarian about the likelihood of FHS:

- While your cat is rushing about, the skin on its back looks to be rippling.
- Even after you've treated your cat for fleas, it bites at its back above its tail regularly.
- Petting your cat's tail or back causes it to groom, scratch, or bite the region excessively before running around the house erratically.

Steps to follow

It's not always easy to figure out what led your cat to go a little crazy all of a sudden. Cats, to be honest, are difficult to decipher! Many people are familiar with fundamental canine vocalizations and actions, but many are unfamiliar with basic cat habits.

Dogs have expressive looks and body language that is quite easy to read. They wag their tails, make various noises to communicate their moods, and frequently obey basic directions to satisfy their owners. On the other hand, Cats are more commonly associated with emotional ambiguity and aloof demeanor. However, there is a growing consensus that cats are as expressive as dogs. 3 People simply misunderstand or fail to notice what or how their cats are attempting to express.

Learn to communicate with your cat

Meows and tail waves can imply various things to cats, depending on the situation. Your cat attempts to communicate with you with each purr, yowl, or even blink. The issue is deciphering what it's saying.

According to experts, there is something to be gained from these efforts at communication. Learning to understand your cat's body language, for example, can help you develop your bond with it and become more adept at reacting to its demands.

Because each cat is unique, simply observing your cat is the best place to begin. Keep a mental record of the place and circumstances in which the "mad" conduct occurs. Take note of your cat's body language, vocalizations, the time of day, and what they have recently done. Has your cat recently eaten, groomed, or scratched its back? Before your cat rushed into the other room, did you hear a playful meow?

You'll likely begin to put together the triggers of your cat's crazy in various scenarios with time and careful observation. This can help you understand what is normal for your cat and when any odd behavior is a sign of a medical problem that your veterinarian should investigate.

Chapter Seven

COMMON ISSUES WITH CATS AT HOME

Train your cat to stop urine marking

Marking behavior is when a cat feels the urge to indicate its territory by urinating outside the box. However, some underlying health disorders and some environmental factors might lead a cat to urinate beyond the litter box.

If this behavior occurs more than once or twice, you should take your cat to the veterinarian to rule out any health problems. If it is, in fact, marking behavior, you can make efforts to stop it.

Making their ground

Cats mark an area that is important to them with urine. Cats often get along nicely until they attain social maturity, which occurs between the ages of 2 and 4. Squatting and depositing urine or feces on a horizontal surface is typical of house-soiling, whereas urine marking is more likely to target vertical surfaces.

On the other hand, Cats can pee on both horizontal and vertical surfaces. Although intact male cats are more likely to spray urine, neutered cats of either sex can choose to baptize the house.

Examine the litter box

Cats will avoid using the litter box if it's in the incorrect place (too close to food or sleeping areas), if it's dirty, or if they have to share it with another cat. They might not want to "go" after another kitten, or they might want a food and liquids box.

Cats have extremely specific preferences for the types of box filters or surfaces, and the box may be too tiny for a big-tailed feline at times.

Stress reduction

Spreading the aroma of urine about the house can actually help cats relax. Cats are creatures of habit, and anything that throws them off can make their tails twitch. It may be anything from new drapes to a stray cat patrolling outside the window to an erratic work schedule.

When stray cats go into heat in the spring, the scent and sound might cause indoor cats to feel more anxious and territorially mark their territory. Furthermore, stress might exacerbate any physical or behavioral issues. So, whether your cat's problem is health-related or purely territorial, a stress-reduction program should assist.

Use Feliway to help you

If you have more than one cat, they may have attained social maturity and are vying for dominance in the house. The Feliway synthetic pheromone can be beneficial since it alerts the cat to the safety of its surroundings. For a small percentage of cats, Rescue Remedy reduces stress.

Remove the odor and form new associations

Keep an eye out for your cat's urine stains. Urine should glow under a black light, allowing you to see any dirty areas plainly. Clean thoroughly with an odor neutralizer, such as Anti-Icky-Poo, to remove the odor that attracts cats to the crime scene (and fragrance). Ammonia and bleach are also effective. The idea is to get rid of the stink so that the cat won't "go" there again.

Then, just on top of the site, install toys, a cat bed, or food bowls to change the place's association. Cats will avoid spraying in areas where they play, sleep, or feed. Spraying Feliway on the offending area can also help prevent a repeat offense.

Add a second litter box

You may need to coddle twice as much if you have numerous cats (or more). Provide at least one litter box per cat, and distribute them throughout the house. Make sure they're extremely large because some cats enjoy having more room to move around.

Likewise, provide scratching objects and resting spots for each cat in various locations throughout the house. Cats can use the extra vertical space to climb and get away from one other, each with its resting location. Single-cat shelves (with only enough space for one cat) can eliminate the need for cats to share.

Problems and proofreading techniques

If you can't stop the spray, see your veterinarian. Kidney disease and diabetes can cause the cat's urine volume to increase, making it impossible to reach the litter box in time.

Bladder stones, crystals, bacterial infection, or malignancy that causes bladder inflammation can all cause feline lower urinary tract disease (FLUTD). Cystitis hurts cats and makes them feel compelled to "go" more frequently. They may link the litter box with discomfort and seek alternative locations to urinate.

Furthermore, 60 percent of these cases are idiopathic, meaning no known cause makes the medical condition challenging to treat. Idiopathic cystitis symptoms usually go away on their own after five to seven days, but they can reoccur, particularly in stressful settings.

Stop destructive chewing in cats

While it's natural for cats to chew on things that aren't meant to be chewed, the activity can sometimes become excessive. It could be dangerous for the cat, as well as damaging to your valuables. On the other hand, Cats gnaw on things because they explore with their mouths. Excessive chewing in cats can be caused by various medical issues, including teething in kittens. However, boredom is the leading cause of chewing in home cats, and it is quite easy to alleviate.

Reasons

Before assuming that your cat's chewing behavior is due to boredom, take it to the doctor to rule out a medical problem. A cat with gum disease may bite on objects to relieve pain, whereas a cat with a digestive problem may chew and spit on objects to relieve nausea.

Medical explanations for chewing include obsessive-compulsive disorder, dietary deficits, and early weaning. Periodontal disease, an inflammation of the gums and surrounding tissues, is quite common in cats and is usually treated with a complete cleaning under anesthesia to remove plaque and tartar, which host bacteria that cause periodontal disease.

Affected teeth may need to be removed in more advanced stages of periodontal disease. A cat with a digestive problem will normally show more indicators than just chewing that it is sick, so how your doctor treats it will depend on the degree and nature of the condition.

If there's no underlying medical cause, you're probably dealing with a bored cat. Although it may not appear that a kitten could get into too much trouble chewing, there are several severe dangers that you may be neglecting around the house.

<u>Steps to follow</u>

Wires and cords, houseplants, and fabric or leather furniture are kittens' most typical chewing objects. Take a slightly different method to keep the cat from gnawing on each object.

- *Cords and Wires*

Cats love to chew on cords and wires, especially if they are left alone throughout the day. Toys that your cat or kitten can swat or bat about on the wall or door, cat towers to investigate with linked toys for added interest, or even an arrangement of cardboard boxes on the floor to form a tunnel with holes cut through the sides are all good options. Treatdispensing toys are a terrific method to satisfy their natural hunting instincts.

To deal with the cord dilemma, you'll need to find a means to cover the cords, prevent access to them, or make them unappealing to gnaw on.

Pre-split hollow tubing for covering cords and electrical wires and kits for handling computer cords are available at many computer supply retailers. Flexible poly tubing comes in various diameters and can be purchased in most building supplies or hardware stores if you're handy with a utility knife. Slit one side of the tubing then cut each cord to length. If larger "corrugated" tubing doesn't work, you could try larger "corrugated" tubing to run several wires through.

Apply several rows of double-sided sticky tape to the floor around a huge cord tangle to prevent access to the cords (such as frequently happens with computers). Walking through the tape will be difficult for cats.

Make the Cords Taste Bad: Bitter apple spray is by far one of the most effective teaching tools for any type of destructive chewing. It will leave a sour taste in your cat's mouth that he will not soon forget. Be aware that if you have a persistent cat, you may need to reapply to the place you wish your cat to avoid.

- *Houseplants*

Your living houseplants may become a target for your cat's natural inclination to nibble on vegetation. Some of these plants are particularly toxic to cats, so you must learn to recognize and avoid them for the sake of your cat's safety.

If any of your houseplants appear on our list of hazardous plants, either eliminate them or make them unavailable to your cat.

- *Items made of fabric and leather*

Wool chewing is classified as an OCD symptom. For the type of chewing activity, we're talking about, the simplest method to discourage it is to provide your cat with other "legal" chewing options, such as chewable soft toys.

If you can't put away all of your cat's favorite fabric and leather goods, try spraying some bitter apple on the area where it chews, but test it first on a little concealed seam to make sure it doesn't stain.

Kittens

Plastic drinking straws, especially the huge ones used for milkshakes, are one item that helps kitties with teething. They offer kitties with the crunchy contact they require while also serving as a fun interactive toy.

Tease your kitten with the straw, then let him "capture" it and watch him proudly carry around his "prey" for hours of interactive fun. Adult cats may recall their straws, so it's not uncommon to see one hitting it about the floor.

Clicker practice

Clicker training is most commonly used with dogs, but it can also be utilized with cats. When the animal accomplishes the required behavior, the trainer or pet owner will create a clicking noise using a small hand-held gadget. To be effective with clicker training, the click must be followed by a treat for the animal to learn to associate the action and the click with a pleasurable experience. The goodie can eventually be phased out.

Do not smack or yell

It's ineffective in most animals, especially cats, who don't correlate poor behavior with the intended negative reinforcement.

Train your cat to walk on a leash

Contrary to popular opinion, Cats may be trained to perform many of the same tasks as dogs. Some cats even love activities such as leash walking. A cat on a leash, like a puppy who has never been leash-trained, will have no idea what to do unless it has been trained to walk on it first.

Collar and harness

Collars are useful for identifying cats and hanging a bell on them, but they aren't ideal for using a leash. Cats have a different build than dogs, and they can easily slip out of a leash-attached collar. Harnesses are safer to walk a cat in, especially when it's still being trained.

Choose a harness for your cat that is safe and snug but not too tight. By putting two fingers underneath the harness, you can ensure it isn't too tight. It should fit properly if two fingers can pass between the harness and your cat. However, it is either too slack or too tight if you can fit more or fewer fingers beneath the harness.

The best harnesses for cats are those that are specifically intended for them. If a harness is too tight or difficult to walk in, your cat will only worry about how uncomfortable it is. Harnesses made of a soft material, cut so that a cat may walk properly, and lightweight are the ideal choices for your cat. Make sure the harness you purchase has a D-ring securely linked to the back, as this is where the leash will be attached.

How to choose a cat leash: 4 to 6-foot long, lightweight leashes are suitable for leash training cats of all sizes. Once a cat has been trained, retractable and longer leashes are OK, but initially, stay to a moderate length and leash weight.

Allow your cat to get used to the harness

Allow your cat to become accustomed to the harness once it has been fitted properly. Allow your cat to sniff it while you feed it goodies.

Keep in mind that the time it takes a cat to get acclimated to wearing a harness varies from one cat to the next. Your cat may not mind wearing a harness at all, or it may take several hours or days for your cat to acclimate. While your cat is wearing the harness, be sure to praise it and give it treats. If your cat is afraid of the harness, don't leave it on for more than a few minutes at a time, but gradually increase the time it spends wearing it each time you put it on. Gradually increase your time in the harness until you can leave it on for an hour. If your cat usually walks while wearing the harness, you're ready to move on to the next stage of leash training.

Allow your cat to become used to the leash.

Attach the leash to the D-ring if your cat does not mind wearing the harness. Allow your cat to pull the leash around in the safety of your house to get used to being attached to it. If your cat is easily startled, you should attach the leash and hold it while letting the cat wander around freely. Some cats are afraid of a leash dragging behind them, and you don't want to make your cat afraid of the leash right away. You can take your cat outside once it has become accustomed to the leash being attached to it.

How to make your cat walk on a leash

Maintain control of the leash and allow your cat to roam freely outside. Treats or toys can be used to entice your cat to walk in the direction you desire. Pulling your cat by the leash is not recommended, but a moderate tug to shift its attention is OK. If your cat is walking in the direction you want it to go, you should reward it with treats regularly.

Your cat will become accustomed to the sights, sounds, scents, and sensations of the outdoors over time and will feel secure in its harness and leash. This may take several days or weeks for some cats, while others will feel more at ease immediately away.

Make sure that your cat is safe

Fleas, ticks, heartworms, and other parasites are more common in cats who spend time outside. Consult your veterinarian about preventative measures to ensure that your cat is safe and protected while spending time outside.

Stay away from items that can shock your cat when you're outside, such as busy roads and barking dogs. Even if a cat has been trained to walk on a leash, it may be scared of going on a future walk due to various scenarios.

When cats don't cover their poop

Isn't it true that cats cover their poop? Certainly not. The primary reason wild cats bury their feces is to keep their existence hidden from potential predators. The other is to demonstrate that they are not posing a threat to more dominant cats. These more dominant cats rarely bury their excrement, instead preferring to leave it on grassy tussocks, which elevate it and make it more visible.

So it appears that a dominating cat in the house is the only reason for a domesticated cat to bury her excrement. On the other hand, Burying feces is a fairly normal cat activity. So why isn't your cat doing it?

Humans pleased

Humans have aided this habit in our domestic cats by carefully selecting (and reproducing) the "clean" ones. Cats who leave their feces out in the open for all to see are not weird; they're simply cats. Ask yourself what else has changed if your cat always has dug-and-covered as regular litter box behavior and now makes a statement with uncovered poop. This could be the cat's way of signaling to other cats (or even a stray outside the window) that the territory is theirs.

Making a declaration of territory

In the wild, dominant cats (such as jaguars, leopards, lions, and tigers) who are vying for territory do not bury their excrement, delivering the message that that location is now theirs. To let other cats—or their owner—know "I am here," a domesticated cat may choose not to bury their excrement. Even if a cat has lived in the same location for a long time, he may not consider it his home. The odor of their feces indicates the presence of that particular cat.

Natural predispositions

Cats who don't cover or leave a deposit outside the box may simply be doing what they're used to. Even though burying excrement is typically demonstrated by the mother cat, some cats never learn to do it.

In fact, one research witnessed female pet cats poop 58 times, with only two instances of the cats attempting to dig a hole first or covering it afterward. Unburied garbage may be used by roaming cats as a sort of marking.

Problems with the litter box

Size does key when it comes to litter boxes. Your cat's litter box may be too small for them to turn around and bury their poop. And, as the adage goes, cats may be picky—perhaps they don't like the feel of the cat litter, or the litter box is too filthy, and they'd prefer not to spend any more time in it. If you think one or both of these things are true, try a different kind of litter or get a bigger litter box.

Medical concerns

There aren't any specific illnesses that will lead your cat to stop burying their excrement, but if your cat is in pain—whether in their paws, while going to the bathroom, or simply in general—it may discourage them from spending more time in the litter box. Also, cats who have just been declawed may want to forgo the interment process.

Stop destructive scratching

Cats clawing furniture and other items in the house is a typical complaint among cat owners. Although this can be aggravating, remember that scratching is a common and natural habit in cats. Even though cats naturally desire to scratch, scratching locations we consider improper, such as our couches and stairwell posts, is considered disruptive behavior. Fortunately, this is something that can be readily avoided and handled.

What causes cats to scratch?

Scratching is a natural cat habit necessary for their physical and emotional well-being. You can avoid damage to your home by understanding your cat's scratching activity.

- *To keep the claw motion required for hunting and climbing:* Cats are natural hunters who seize and hold prey with their claws. They also use this action to keep the muscles in their forelimbs and spine in good shape for hunting.

- *Defense and offense:* Cats use their claws to defend themselves when they fight with other cats or other animals.

- *Scratching serves as an emotional release for cats*, who scratch to relieve tension and scratch when excited or aroused. Have you ever witnessed your cat move slowly past another cat in your house before scratching? Scratching is a way for the cat to let off steam. Have you ever seen your cat clawing as soon as you get home from work? Scratching can be a joyful emotion; thus, it's out of eagerness in this situation.

- *It is a sort of exercise that strengthens and expands their muscles:* Scratching is a fantastic kind of exercise for your cats and keeps them in shape. They can lengthen and retract their nails and stretch out their body. Like many of us, cats enjoy stretching first thing in the morning.

- *Cats scratch to communicate with other cats and to mark their territory.* They leave a fragrance and visible traces when they scratch. Their paw pads contain scent glands that leave odors behind when they scratch, alerting other cats to their presence. Cats scratching objects leave minor gouges that serve as visual cues to other cats in the area.

- *Nail care for cats*: When your cat scratches something, the outer dead sheath of the nail is removed, revealing the healthy new growth beneath. Crescent moon-shaped nail sheaths are widespread around your cat's favorite scratching locations.
- *Fun:* Cats enjoy stretching, scratching, and playing!

<u>What can I do to stop my cat scratching?</u>

You can't, to put it bluntly. Scratching is a normal part of your cat's behavior. It's unrealistic to expect this conduct to go away on its own. Scratching is a regular and spontaneous habit for cats, and we must give proper avenues for them to express and feel it.

Punishing your cat for scratching is not a good idea. This includes squirting water, shaking a can of pennies, and other similar activities. Punishment does not teach the proper cat behavior, and it can raise fear, anxiety, stress and harm your relationship with your cat.

Scratching is a natural behavior for cats, so we want to give them appropriate outlets for this behavior by scratching surfaces. Always provide your cat with a variety of acceptable scratching spots with a diversity of surfaces and textures. Scratchers are available in a variety of shapes, sizes, and materials.

To figure out which substrates and scratchers your cat favors, try a range of them. Scratching posts or pads made of sisal rope, cardboard, wood, or sisal fabric are some examples of what most cats enjoy. It's ideal if you can provide both horizontal and vertical scratching surfaces. Scratchers should be strong and not unsteady or tip over when scratched by your cat. Scratching posts for cats must be tall. To receive a full-body stretch, your cat should be able to stand on their hind legs and fully extend their body up the side of the post.

The location of scratchers is crucial. Our cats prefer to be around us, so keep them in settings where you and your cats both spend time. When cats wake up, they tend to stretch or scratch, so consider placing one near where they sleep. When cats are in a difficult environment or trying to relieve anxiety, they scratch. Scratchers should be placed in all areas where you think your cats would appreciate them the most.

Provide appropriate scratching areas

Holding your cat near the scratching post and forcing her to drag her claws on it is not a good idea. We don't like being pushed to do things, and cats are no exception. This may frighten your cat, causing them to avoid the scratcher entirely.

Make the scratching spots you want the cat to scratch more enticing instead. Place catnip or silvervine near them, or attach toys to the scratching post to do this. You may also give your cats food and play with them on or around the scratcher to help them develop a positive relationship with it.

Finally, Feliscratch can be used because one of the reasons cats scratch is to communicate through fragrance. Feliscratch is a Feliway product that imitates the aroma that cats spread to other cats when they scratch. Feliscratch encourages your cats to scratch there again by imitating their messages.

Redirect positively

If your cat is scratching your furniture, figure out their favorite scratching scenario by observing where your cat scratches inappropriately. Is it horizontal or vertical? Vertical? What substrate does it resemble the most? Cardboard? Wood?

Buy scratching posts or pads that are similar to your cat's preferred scratching setup based on their preferences. Place a good scratching post near an unacceptable object based on your cat's preferences (for example, couch). When your cat consistently uses the scratching post, you can gradually move it to a more convenient area (no more than a few inches every day). However, it's important to keep the proper scratching objects as close as possible to your cat's favored scratching spots.

Scratching should be reinforced

Reward your cat with a treat, verbal praise, or a pet when they scratch their scratchers. Remember that what one cat finds reinforcing may not be the same as what another cat finds reinforcing, so praise your cat in a way that they appreciate.

Claw trimming regularly

Because claws don't naturally wear down, your cat must groom them by scratching a rough surface, such as your furniture or carpeting. Regular toenail cutting keeps her nails from becoming snagged and ripped on things and prevents destructive clawing.

Wait patiently and be ready

Take a deep breath and maintain a nice and calm demeanor. Purchase cat nail trimmers that are comfortable to hold, with a rubberized coating to prevent slipping, and a stainless steel blade before you begin.

Make yourself at home

Cut your cat's nails in a peaceful, distraction-free environment. A non-slip surface, such as a yoga mat, is essential for cats to stand on. When cutting your cat's nails, it's better to do so when they are relaxed, rather than in the middle of a game.

Take one step at a time

At the same moment, clip one nail and provide a treat. If your cat remains calm, clip the second nail as it eats; if your cat remains calm, work up to trimming five nails in one sitting. Be prepared to only clip one paw, or possibly one or two claws, at first until your cat gets used to it.

Make it a positive experience

Most cats' experiences with nail trims have been negative, resulting in cats disliking nail trims. Before you begin, prepare some delectable, one-of-a-kind treats that your cats only get during nail trims. Canned food, whip cream, tuna fish, and anchovy paste are just a few examples. Depending on your cat's preferences, you can also give them a cuddle, brush, or play session afterward.

Avoid the hasty

The quick is a pink portion of a cat's nail higher up. Because it includes all of your cat's nerves and blood arteries, cutting into it will cause pain and bleeding. It's easy to see where the quick begins when trimming the nails, so you don't nick it. If you cut it by accident, you can quickly stop the bleeding using styptic powder.

Ask for assistance

If your cat is averse to having her claws trimmed or having her paws handled, a trained professional can assist you in teaching your cat to tolerate and even love nail clipping.

Enriching the environment

Enrichment is vital for cats because a boring environment can lead to destructive scratching and other behavioral disorders; therefore, it's important to supply them with it. Enriching your cat's environment allows them to express these behaviors. An enriched environment should include a range of scratching surfaces, outlets for predatory and prey behavior, safe locations, and an environment that allows an animal to have various choices and control over their daily activities.

The challenge of declawing

Scratching is a natural action beneficial to your cat's physical and emotional health. Cat claws originate from the last bone in their toes, unlike human nails, which sprout from the flesh. Declawing (onychectomy) is the amputation of this bone, as well as the tendons, nerves, and ligaments that connect it to the rest of the body. It's a significant surgery that might leave your cat vulnerable to a range of physical and behavioral issues. Declawing is outlawed in many nations worldwide because it is deemed inhumane.

Chapter Eight
TRAVELING WITH YOUR CAT

The majority of people despise the idea of taking their cats on vacation or a road trip. A few bold felines don't mind traveling, but leaving their usual surroundings and traveling can be terrifying for most cats. On the other hand, traveling with a cat is achievable without a great deal of difficulty. The trick is to plan ahead of time by progressively acclimating your cat to travel and gathering supplies well before the departure date.

Traveling by car

Prepare your pet for travel. Take your cat on several brief car rides if it hasn't been in a car in a while, several weeks before your vacation (30 minutes or less). To get the cat acquainted with the noise and action of the automobile, as well as the smell of the cage, place it in the travel cage you'll be using on your journey.

While your cat is in the car, give it some snacks. It will have a better sensation about being there as a result of this. Consider these practice runs to iron out any kinks before you go on a long journey far from home.

If necessary, get motion sickness medicine on prescription. Ask your vet to prescribe medicine if your cat is prone to motion sickness, which your trial runs should reveal. Motion sickness can be controlled with anti-nausea medications like chlorpromazine.

Crying or vocalizing that doesn't stop after a few minutes in the car, excessive drooling, immobility, acting afraid to move, excessive activity or pacing, vomiting, or urinating or defecating are all indicators of motion sickness in cats.

Ginger has also been used to cure nausea in people and is harmless for cats; it can be purchased in liquid or chew form from online or brick-and-mortar pet retailers, as well as from the occasional veterinarian clinic.

Give your cat the Bach Flower Essence "Rescue Remedy" to help it cope with travel-related anxiety and stress, as well as a dread of new environments.

If it is clearly disturbed, put a few drops in his water and a drop in his mouth before leaving each day. Give an oral dose and then go on a short automobile ride 30 minutes later to see how effective it is. Sedatives will merely slow a cat down; however, floral essence will help them stay calm and confident.

As a final option, get prescription tranquilizers. Before turning to drugs, start with trial drives and non-medicated choices. Your veterinarian can assist you in determining which option is best for your cat. Antihistamines (Benadryl) and prescription medications, such as alprazolam (Xanax), are two possibilities for anxiety relief. Discuss dosages with your veterinarian for the greatest results, and heed their advice.

A few days before your vacation, try any sedatives at home. Observe the cat's behavior, and if any bad outcomes emerge, contact your veterinarian to alter dosages or try a new treatment. Varied medications have different effects on cats, just like they do on people. If your pet exhibits irritability or other negative symptoms, your veterinarian will most likely recommend an alternative treatment.

Most sedatives aren't strong enough to knock the cat out completely, but they can help. Before you leave, tell your veterinarian if the medicine is too sedating or not sedating enough. Even when on the sedative, the cat should remain aware of its surroundings.

Put the cat in the carrier and go for a drive while on the drug trial. This way, you'll be prepared for what to expect when traveling with a medicated cat. Make sure your veterinarian provides you with adequate medication for the duration of your trip (both to and from) and request an additional pill or two to try at home before you go.

A few days before the trip, get a towel or blanket and place it in your cat's bed or wherever it likes to sleep. The idea is to get your cat's and your home's scents onto the towel. Furthermore, the cat will be familiar with the towel and will seek comfort from it.

Prepare the cage the night before or the morning of the journey. Put the towel your cat has been lying on at the bottom of the cage, and if the cage floor needs more padding, put another towel under the cage. Include a favorite toy to keep your cat entertained.

Twenty minutes before you're ready to travel, spray Feliway inside the carrier and car. It should keep your cat calm during the journey. Before spraying Feliway in the carrier, make sure to test your cat's reaction to it. A small percentage of cats mistake the spray for the markings of another cat and have a negative or even hostile reaction to it. This is similar to the pheromones that cats emit when they're at ease in their territory.

Traveling by plane

Examine the rules governing airlines. Check all of the many aspects of flying with your cat when booking your journey. Check with the airline to see if your cat may fly in the cabin with you or if she'll have to fly in the cargo hold below deck. Some airlines do not allow animals to travel onboard planes. Depending on your scenario, you and your cat may have to board separate flights.

Flying in the cargo hold might be exceedingly risky for some cat species. It's not suggested for Persian cats, for example, who have brachycephalic facial features, or "smushed faces." It's difficult to breathe in that part of the plane because of their tiny nasal passages.

Select a direct flight and double-check your ticket details. Try to book a direct ticket to cut down on travel time, as connecting and connecting flights can take longer. You'll probably appreciate the shorter route as well. Check your cat's ticket details against your own before taking off. Make sure that every tag linked to your cat's carrier has both your flight and contact information properly written on it.

A 24-hour feeding schedule should also be attached to your cat's carrier. This manner, if your cat is delayed in her travels, she will be looked for.

Use a soft-shell carrier if possible. Check with the airline to see whether you may bring your cat in a carrier and whether it needs to be hard or soft. If your cat has to fly in the cargo hold, the airline may require a specific type. Your cat may be able to fly in the cabin with you in some instances. A soft-shell carrier will be easy to stow under the seat for takeoff and landing if this is the case.

If your cat is flying in the cargo hold, a hard-shell carrier is recommended.

Consider the cargo hold's surroundings. Consider your cat's comfort if she will be flying in the cargo hold. Consider the weather in the area, the season, and the time of day you'll be flying. To avoid the heat in the cargo hold during the hot summer months, fly early in the morning or overnight. Flying in the afternoon during the frigid winter months is usually more comfortable.

Many airlines will not allow your cat to fly in the cargo hold if the weather is likely to be extremely hot. Another reason to check with the airline before flying is to avoid surprises.

Holidays with cats

Summer has finally arrived! Summer weekend trips and longer holidays are starting to happen as we begin to cautiously travel again during COVID-19. So, how's your kitty doing? Is your cat going to accompany you on your trip, or would he prefer to stay at home?

Cats, on the whole, love routine and predictability. Your cat may enjoy being with you, but traveling to odd new areas might cause stress in your cat, which can lead to illness or behavioral issues. On the other hand, I know several cats who regularly like traveling with their people. Their personality determines your cat's reaction to travel.

Taking your cat on a short journey could end up doing more harm than good. A brief trip would not give your cat enough time to settle in and acclimate to the new environment. As a result, the amount of stress they'd be under could be considerable. If your cat is at home in his familiar surroundings, being pampered by a trusted friend or pet sitter, you'll be able to relax and enjoy your holiday more.

If, on the other hand, you're going away for a few weeks or even the entire summer, you'll undoubtedly want to bring your favorite feline companion along for the ride. While it may be stressful for your cat at first, it is preferable for them to come along than to be without you for an extended amount of time.

I've relocated (too) many times with my cats, and I've successfully driven many cats across the nation twice, covering over 2500 miles each time. Whether you're traveling for a vacation or relocating across the nation as I did, these travel suggestions can help you, and your cat enjoys the summer together and make vacationing with your cat as stress-free as possible.

Shy Cats vs. Bold Cats

If you have a kitten or a young cat, you may have to deal with some feline worry. By nature, kittens are bold, while young adult cats are more adaptive. As a result, they are better at traveling than their older counterparts. Adult cats naturally lively and inquisitive may also cope well with travel.

However, if you have a shy cat or are aggressive when meeting new people or in unfamiliar situations, taking him on a journey would most likely be upsetting for both of you.

Preparation for travel

It's a good idea to get a sense of how well your cat will manage a car ride ahead of time. Short car rides are a good way to get your cat used to both being in his carrier and being in motion. This will allow you and Kitty to be more prepared, making the vacation more enjoyable for both of you.

Put your cat in a safe carrier and take him on short rides so that his first vehicle travel isn't a multi-day adventure. These short car excursions will familiarize him with being inside the carrier in a moving vehicle, even if you're flying. When your cat sees that he will ultimately be let out of the carrier, these shorter journeys will help him feel less anxious.

It's a good idea to write your name and phone number on the cat carrier if you are separated from your cat during the travel. This is especially critical if you're flying and might get separated at the security checkpoint or the baggage claim area.

If your cat hasn't been microchipped yet, now is the time to do so. If they don't already, it's also a good idea to get them used to wearing a collar and tag. Your name and phone number should be on the tag, so you can be reached quickly if your cat gets separated from you on the way or runs away once you arrive at your location. You should also get your cat used to walking on a leash and wearing a harness. Some cats appreciate this, and it's a safe method for a kitty to stretch his legs during a long car ride.

Take your cat to the vet for a check-up as soon as possible before your vacation, as several airlines and even state border crossings demand a travel certificate before your cat can enter. It's also a good idea to get a copy of your cat's medical records to bring with you in case they need veterinarian attention while you're away. Research veterinarians in your vacation destination ahead of time so you'll be prepared if the need arises.

During the Journey

There are several things you can do to help your trip to your vacation destination go as well as possible. Feed your cat only in the evenings when on vacation, after you've finished your day's journey and are settled in for the night. This will reduce the likelihood of motion sickness during the trip, and it won't kill him if he skips breakfast for a day or two. Make sure he drinks plenty of water and keeps hydrated.

Adding herbal calming essences to your cat's water can help him stay calm. There are a variety of over-the-counter holistic medicines available, and you may contact your veterinarian for assistance in selecting the correct one for your cat. Using a pheromone spray or plug-in when resting in the evening during a multi-day journey and at your ultimate destination may also help the kitty feel calm.

Keep the cat carrier locked and secured at all times when driving. If you're driving and need to open the carrier to attach a leash, clean up a spill, or just to reassure kitty, do it with all the car doors closed and locked, as well as all the windows rolled up, to avoid an unintentional cat escape.

If you're traveling, make sure to use an airport-approved carrier and double-check with your airline ahead of time to see if pets are permitted onboard. Avoid putting your cat in the luggage compartment beneath the plane, where accidents can (and do) occur. In addition, the baggage hold is not as comfortable as the passenger cabin because it is not pressurized or heated/cooled.

If you're driving and staying at a pet-friendly hotel, don't open the door to the outside once your cat has emerged from his carrier, or he may dash away. Check the room for potential escape dangers and hiding spots, such as under-bed springs, inside a chair, holes in the wall, and so on, before releasing your cat out of his carrier.

You've arrived at your destination

Bravo! You've arrived at your vacation destination. The tricky part is finished, and now it's time to familiarize your cat with his new "home away from home" so he can begin to unwind.

Begin by placing his carrier in a small room, such as a den or bathroom, so that he may become accustomed to the new sights and smells without becoming overwhelmed. Check for any potential escape routes, such as sagging screens or open windows or doors. Encourage him to exit the carrier by chatting softly and presenting him with some of his favorite treats. Allow him to go at his own pace.

Bringing any of your cat's items with you, such as his cat bed, toys, and cat bowls, will assist him in acclimating to his new environment. It will provide your cat a sense of security to have things from home that already smell like him and like home. Also, continue giving him the same cat food brand as you used at home. If your cat has a sensitive stomach, giving him bottled water or using a filtered water pitcher may be a brilliant idea. A new city's water could irritate his stomach (and yours as well).

Your cat will soon be comfortable and napping in your lap, delighted to be spending this special moment with you. Cats ultimately adjust to new environments and are content to simply be with you, no matter where you are. It's enough to make your cat purr with delight as long as you're together.

Vacation and separation anxiety in cats

Vacations are designed to be enjoyable for people, but they can be stressful for cats because of the change in routine, resulting in behavior issues and separation anxiety. Cat behavior issues might arise when the owner is away, during transportation, or after the owner returns. While some cats can handle traveling, staying in hotels, or being kept in a kennel, the majority of cats are best off with a pet sitter in their own home. Of course, this isn't always possible, but there are some things you can do to reduce your cat's stress and the possibility of behavior problems around the holidays.

Environmental changes in your cat's life

Cats adore and thrive on routine, to the point where any disruption can lead them to become agitated. Many things change for cats when their owners go on vacation, including the absence of their owners, different feeding times, less attention, new persons, and, in certain cases, new habitats if they are boarded.

It can take your cat anywhere from five days to two weeks—and often even longer—to adjust to and accept a new schedule. Consider how long some cats take to accept additional cats into their household or to acclimatize to a new environment. Both of these scenarios highlight how unyielding cats can be. A stranger who does not follow the schedule, such as a pet sitter, adds stress to your cat's life. When your cat has adjusted to the new pattern with the pet sitter, you will return from vacation and alter their daily routine once more. Your cat hasn't been able to refresh their cheek-rub patterns while you've been gone, so you don't smell recognizable to them. As a result, some cats will hide, become protective, or engage in undesirable behavior.

Urinating outside the box

When there is a change in the family, one of the most prevalent behavior problems noticed in cats is inappropriate elimination, particularly urinating outside the litter box.

Cats may act aggressively or fearfully toward unfamiliar pet caregivers or in unfamiliar situations such as boarding facilities. To communicate that they are worried or stressed, kittens may urinate outside their litter box. Because cats enjoy the aroma of their urine, marking their territory helps them relax by spreading their scent onto items that smell like their owner. Urine is difficult to remove from goods such as furniture, carpeting, and mattresses, making dealing with and cleaning it up frustrating.

Excessive scratching

When cats are agitated or stressed, they may scratch more, in addition to urinating inappropriately. Scratching is a natural action that they utilize to keep their claws healthy and identify their territory. However, during stressful periods for your cat, this behavior may intensify and become a concern.

Cats' hiding behavior

Cats are typically terrified of new things, and if they are, they will hide. Your cat's fear of the scenario causes him to hide from the pet sitter, at a boarding facility, and even when you return home.

Cats' attacking behavior

When cats are terrified or agitated, they may react violently or defensively. This can be seen in cats who are stressed out because they are in a new scenario or setting. Cats' fear and stress can manifest in swatting, hissing, lunging, and biting.

Vacations and stress reduction in cats

There are a few things cat owners may do in advance of a vacation to make it easier for their cat:

If your cat stays at home while you are away, have the pet sitter meet them as many times as possible before you go. Your cat's favorite treats should be offered, and the pet sitter should play with them and their favorite toys. This will assist your cat in associating the pet sitter with a positive and enjoyable experience. Allow your cat to run away if they so desire. Do not confine them to force a meeting.

Bring out your suitcase at least a week ahead of time to allow your cat to become accustomed to it. To make a pleasant association for the cat anytime, they see your luggage, toss in some treats or toys. If you need to move your cat, this also applies to your cat carrier.

Make a list of your daily schedule and have the pet sitter stick to it. Meals, playing, grooming, lap-sitting interactions, and other critical benchmarks should all be adhered to as strictly as possible to keep your cat as stress-free as possible. If you know the routine will alter while you're gone, make some of the modifications a few days before you go so the cat can start adjusting without the added stress of your absence.

Leave a fragrance item for your cat, such as a t-shirt that you've worn but not washed. Leaving this in your cat's bed can make them feel better. Some cats will love your recorded voice/message being played while you're away, while others will grow upset, so try it out before you go.

Before you go, have each member of your family who loves your cat pick a pair of socks from their closet. Rub the socks all over the cat before putting each pair in its plastic bag. When you get home from your vacation, put on the cat-scented socks so you may carry the cat's characteristic identification that "you are family" once more.

If you're going to board your cat, bring some of their favorite toys or snacks, as well as items that smell like you, to the facility. If the facility allows it, try to get them to follow your typical feeding and playtime schedules. Tell the staff about your cat's favorite activities or places to be petted, and if you must transfer your cat, do so in a container covered with a towel. Play quiet music in the car to keep them calm, and secure the carrier with a seat belt or on the vehicle's floor. In the carrier, you can also place some sweets or favorite foods.

For cats with stress and anxiety, medications, nutritional supplements, and pheromones are all options. Many of these tasks should be completed before leaving on vacation and can be really beneficial.

CONCLUSION

If you've never had a cat before but sense a kitty-shaped void in your life, you should consider your expectations carefully. Do you expect your cat to sleep on your lap while you read, use the litter box automatically, or not harm the birds that frequent your bird feeder? What do you know about cat behavior, or think you know about it?

Expectations rarely match reality. It's crucial to keep in mind that the lazy fat cat of your fantasies might not be the cat you end up with.

Cats can be very self-reliant, but only on their terms, and some days may be more self-reliant than others. Your cat may spend two days outside, catching frogs, resting in the shed, and slinking away whenever you enter the room. Then she'll follow you into the restroom, tripping you up as she snakes between your legs. She only needs her ears stroked on some days. If you even try to touch her side, she'll fight you tooth and nail.

When most cats desire affection, they make it clear. They make it clear when they aren't in the mood for caressing. You'll get more attuned to your cat's whims the longer you share your home with her. You'll be able to tell whether she's having a nice day or a don't-touch-me diva moment rather quickly.

Some cats have a natural quiet time when they don't want to be disturbed, such as at sunset, when you'll observe your cat perched at a window or on a rooftop watching the sunset in utter calm, and at sunrise when all the birds and small critters in your yard begin preparing for the day.

Make no mistake: having a cat as a companion is fantastic. However, just because cats are more independent than dogs doesn't mean you can sit back and enjoy while they take care of themselves. It is not true that if you want to go away for the weekend, you will have no problems. It's also not true that a pet cat can survive on its own, allowing you to leave them alone for the weekend.

By putting everything you've learned through this guide into practice, you can make your life as a cat parent more enjoyable. Once you get to know your cat - and thanks to this book, this process will definitely be easier - you won't be able to part with it.

Have a great life and meow!

www.ingramcontent.com/pod-product-compliance
Lightning Source LLC
Chambersburg PA
CBHW071520080526
44588CB00011B/1508